Foreward

Thoughts tumbled around in my brain for years. I set about the business of writing them down and then as stories turned to pages and pages to chapters I realized I was writing a book. But when I sat down to make the book happen I ran into fear. Once I pushed back against the fear and found my faith I realized I could be brave. However, once I reached the point of bravery, this thing called "self-doubt" crept in. Cause as I've learned from Brené Brown, bravery is actually vulnerability. So I found myself back in a place of fear. The cycle continued.

There were women, brave, honest, vulnerable women, who rode this roller coaster of fear-faith-bravery and vulnerability with me from start to finish. Women who prayed for me, cried with me, and encouraged me. From the gift of dropping off emergency scones, to sharing tears on the floor of my sunroom with me, these women held my arms steady when I was too weak, unwilling, or wandering in my faith to finish this book. These women were my faithful warriors—never taking glory, but deserving of it all the same. It seems only fitting they would pave the way for this book. Here is what they have to say about *Chin Up*:

"Even if you might be unsure of where you stand spiritually, do not doubt your decision to buy this book. We can ALL, as mothers, relate to Amy's perspective on mothering because Amy is relatable and real. Like hanging out with your best friend who is trying to reassure you of the amazing job you are doing as a mom, Amy's words will lift you up, make you laugh, and give you grace. What mom doesn't need that?"
—Holly Galligan

"If every mom read this book, we would have a world of moms fully rested, deeply secured, and entirely grace-covered. Amy's honesty cuts through charades, her words hunt for Jesus like He's an actual treasure, and her delivery of new perspectives reminds us of the things that matter most. After reading this book,

I wanted to linger a little longer with my kid on the floor, stay in my pj's for a couple more hours, and change a couple more diapers in the name of love."
—Lori Brittenham

"Right in the middle of my overwhelming and underwhelming moments of motherhood, Amy's words have been sweet encouragement and needed truth. As she transparently shared her journey toward a motherhood of more grace, I found myself underlining and amen-ing, laughing about motherhood, and mostly, shifting my eyes and heart towards Jesus."
—Trinity Gawron

"Amy asks the questions we are all asking inside, but dare not say aloud. Relatable, hopeful, and funny, *Chin Up* will help you to take a deep breath and find peace in the mother you were designed to be.
—Sara Martin

"Lovely. Full of grace and His Word and pointers to find Him. Wish the young mom me could have read this. So much grace."
—Sandy Rieske

"*Chin Up* is a pocketful of grace for the imperfect mom. As a parent of a special needs child, it is a solid reminder to embrace and accept my weaknesses, admit my failures, and turn my *Chin Up* to regain perspective, accept God's grace, and serve the King by loving my little people."

—Erin Kessler

"I wish I had understood how much I got in my own way as a young mother. How my expectations and misguided focus of what was really important was souring the good harvest I was laboring towards. *Chin Up* has been a refreshing guide pointing towards God's truth about my labor as a mother. Each chapter has given me freedom and grace to bring myself under the council of the master gardener."

—Jamie Alt

"Amy's refreshing words pour grace and truth into some of the most unattractive nooks and crannies of motherhood."

—Jenn Squizzato

"Amy pulls up a chair and sits right next to you in the middle of the loneliest, and most complicated parts of motherhood. In *Chin Up* she puts her arm around you, considers you precious, lets you cry, makes you laugh, and then helps you get up off the floor and not only survive motherhood, but give a twirl feeling confident, beautiful, and covered by grace amidst all the chaos."

—Gelly May

"Young mothers need a shoulder to cry on, the truth of God's grace, and the type of laughter that reminds them—chin up, you are not alone. Amy Seiffert's words offer all of this and more in a voice that needs to be heard. Her wisdom and vulnerability are a gift."

—Libby Romanin

Chin Up

Wearing Grace, Strength, and Dignity
When Motherhood Unravels Our Souls

AMY SEIFFERT

PUBLISHING

South Main Publishing

Chin Up
Copyright © 2017 by Amy Seiffert

ISBN-13: 978-1976398094

ISBN-10: 1976398096

Cover design: Rob Seiffert
Cover photo: Rob Wagner
Author photo: Suzy Dally Schumacher

Written on my iPhone, voice-text, and kid fingerprint stained laptop. Between laundry folding, lunch prep, and half taken naps. Please excuse any typos and grammatical oversights. While hundreds of eyeballs have read this multiple times, nobody's perfect. If there's anything I'm sure of—there's grace for this too.

First printing October 2017 / Printed in the United States of America

For my Dad, who said it without thinking.
For my circus, who I adore and wear grace for daily:
Robby, Olive, Judah
For my husband, who said: Let's do this. You're
always game. Always encouraging. Always mine.

Contents

Introduction XV

1. Gifts & Grace 1

2. Shift to See the Gift........................... 11

3. Maintaining and Sustaining.............. 23

4. The Spirituality of Motherhood....... 31

5. Four Things 39

6. Growing Oaks.................................... 45

7. Step Outside 53

8. Beauty Instead of Ashes 61

9. On Anger and Acorns 71

10. Two Callings, One Roof.................... 83

11. I Will Fight for You 95

12. The Good Part 107

13. Dear Mom at Target 117

14. Orphans 125

15. I'm Bringing Sabbath Back 135

16. How Fitting 147

From the Author 153

Acknowledgments 157

Discussion Questions.......................... 163

Notes 173

Introduction

I kept waking up each morning with the same thought: "I don't think I can climb this mountain called Today. Again." My view of motherhood was both overwhelming and underwhelming. And I was tired of fighting with myself, with the clock, with my tribe. I longed to shift to see the gifts in front of me.

One of these mornings as I was willing myself out of bed, my Dad's soft words came to mind: "Chin up."

He said this to my sister and I when we were growing up and "catastrophe" had struck. It wasn't a statement out of frustration from him. It wasn't a call to shake it off or tough it out. Just the opposite. It was a reminder, said in gentleness, about standing back up and changing our perspective.

When we focus on our issues and our messy world

and our failures we fail to look up and see beyond ourselves. We easily lose perspective and we lose the call of the King: Chin up, Dear One.

But you, O Lord, are a shield about me, my glory, and the lifter of my head.

—*Psalm 3:3*

And I've come to know there is hope here, right here in my kitchen and my deadlines and my tired body and my perfectionism. We can hear God say:

Chin up, it's not that bad.

Chin up, it is that bad, but I am standing here with you.

Chin up, there is a time to grieve and a time to be brave. Let's know the difference.

Chin up, you blew it big time but I make beauty from ashes.

Chin up, things are so much bigger than you.

Thank God.

This one is for those who long to shift their perspective in the middle of motherhood. In the middle of anger. In the middle of two callings under one roof. In the middle of life. In our everyday lives we can shift our perspective and trust that God is with us and for us.

Mother \ muhth-er \ noun
1. One person who does the work of twenty. For free. (See also: 'masochist', 'loony', 'saint')

"Experience: the most brutal of teachers. But you learn, my God do you learn."
—C.S. Lewis

1

Gifts & Grace

"I just want to grow up and be a mom," one of my best friends, Kati, dreamed out loud. We were third-graders in our pj's at a sleepover. The slew of us girls on the bedroom floor, matchmaking marriages, painting nails, and playing Mall Madness with its on-the-fritz battery. We were sharing dreams.

But I didn't chime in on the motherhood dream. I loved my mom and the moms of all my friends. They were kind, funny, creative, and honest. Moms, overall, were working out well in my little world. I just had other ideas. And so did they, of course. All those beautiful third grade girls grew up to become women with college degrees, work various jobs, build careers, and yes, become mothers. In all honesty, motherhood never really crossed my mind much. Art, athletics, moving to California, writing, and creating things occupied my mind. Instead of babysitting for a summer job, I mowed lawns. I didn't know what I wanted to do, but I wanted to do something amazing and change the world and leave a mark.

I was always dreaming. Now, three decades later and ten years into motherhood, with three beautiful souls under my roof, I find myself accomplishing some of the dreams birthed in my heart as a young girl. I also find myself a mother. And motherhood, many days, feels like pushing sand uphill.

About a year into motherhood I found myself frustrated under the weight of "being mom" to my sweet son. My days revolved around mundane tasks, an uninspiring list of chores to accomplish, continual disaster clean up and tantrum management. My view of motherhood was hardly inspiring. Everywhere I looked, motherhood looked beautiful on women. However, on me motherhood felt like a lopsided dress. Each time I tried to adjust it, I exposed another part of me I wanted covered. Why couldn't I get motherhood to "fit" on me? What was I doing wrong?

Something needed to shift.

Was it me? Was it my kids? Was it my part-time job? Was it my view of the world? Was it my view of God? All of it?

If motherhood was the creation of life, why did motherhood feel like it was sucking the life from me?

If the mother was the care taker of the home, why did I feel like I could not stay in control of anything?

If God equips us for our callings, why did I feel so ill-equipped?

So began the hunt. I found myself searching for understanding while sitting in counseling offices, and on girlfriends' couches with Dairy Queen, and taking theology classes to chip away at my contorted view of motherhood.

It's been quite a decade of discovery, disaster, and delight. Motherhood ain't for the weak. I've discovered, as a mother, where I anchor my trust is crucial to my view of motherhood. When it's myself, I'm forced to carry a massive amount of pressure. When I anchor my trust to my emotions, then this ship is sunk. I don't make a very good anchor with my waves of emotion and my capsizing reality. When I anchor my trust in other relationships, no one can stand the weight of my need.

Control is another key player in my view of motherhood. When I grab for control, I squeeze out sweet small people to make houses appear happy. I trade tiny hearts for tidy houses, thinking cleanliness really is close to godliness. But it's not.

Outer cleanliness can cover up some serious inside dirt.

My faulty perspective of motherhood was because I was focusing my eyes on myself. Who I was as a mother, what I could accomplish, or how well I could parent. Turns out shifting perspective can only happen when you have somewhere else to look. I needed a higher mountain, a majestic scene; I needed to look at the big picture.

I needed to see beyond myself and rest in the grandeur of a Good, Mighty King and His Kingdom. And I needed to be able to do it in the middle of changing a diaper. I couldn't afford a daily retreat away by the sea; my children couldn't afford my daily absence.

So what do we find when we lift our chin up to see the King's plan for motherhood? What do we discover when we search out God's grand story?

We find God is a strong shepherd who has gifts just for moms.

I remember being bone-tired and sleepless because my babies resisted sleep like it was their job. I was overwhelmed by the demands of nursing, rocking, shushing. I was underwhelmed by my doughy, stretched out body. And I read this in the middle of the Bible:

Tell the towns of Judah,
"Your God is coming!"

Yes, the Sovereign Lord is coming in power.
He will rule with a powerful arm.
See, he brings his reward with him as he comes.
He will feed his flock like a shepherd.
He will carry the lambs in his arms,
holding them close to his heart.
He will gently lead the mother sheep with their young.
—Isaiah 40:9–11

I loved the sound of "Your God is coming!" It felt like a call out to the weary. To those who wondered if their God had left them. To those who were sleepless and wrestling.

I soaked in the shepherd imagery of God with His flock of people. He specifically wants those who have young to know He will feed them, carry them, hold them close, and gently lead them.

Like a sheep being tapped by the Shepherd's staff it hit me—He was talking to me as a mom!

Desperate to find more strength as a mother I began to search this out in other translations, and found the wording a balm to my soul. "He will gently lead the nursing ewes. The female sheep. Those with young" (NASB).

He is making SURE moms know He has gifts of grace for them. As true as these words were thousands of years ago, they are true today. God has a tenderhearted grace for mothers.

Can we just pause at the word grace? It has changed my life, and the actual word needs special attention. Because it's loaded, and it's significant, and it fills in all the gaps of all of our mess.

Grace: God's favor on the unworthy.

Grace: kindness from God we do not deserve.

Grace: a gift given where nothing is owed in return.

From the beginning, grace was given to bridge the gaps. So many gaps. Gaps between God and us. Gaps between us and others. Gaps in our lives. Gaps in our motherhood.

I desperately needed to shift my eyes to see the gift of grace in front of me. God was whispering, "Chin up, there is grace here for you." So I opened God's Word, and hunted down grace, and found some gems to anchor my soul:

> *The LORD is gracious and merciful; Slow to anger*
> *and great in loving kindness.*
> *—Psalm 145:8*

> *Therefore the LORD longs to be gracious to you,*
> *And therefore He waits on high to have compassion*
> *on you. For the LORD is a God of justice; How*
> *blessed are all those who long for Him.*
> *—Isaiah 30:18*

> *But He gives a greater grace. Therefore it says,*

"God is opposed to the proud, but gives grace to the humble."
—James 4:6

For by grace you have been saved through faith.
And this is not your own doing; it is the gift of God,
not a result of works, so that no one may boast.
—Ephesians 2:8

God's favor and kindness were on me in the middle of my motherhood. In the middle of my frustration, my impatience, my yelling, my chaotic, unorganized heart.

But I didn't believe it.

What I actually believed was I was in control, and the whole mothering thing was up to me. Sure, there was an occasional gift of kindness, but it wasn't the water in which I swam. It wasn't the air I breathed. Grace from God wasn't my lifeline.

Until I started to give up.

I remember looking around the house seeing disorder and obnoxiously colored toys while changing a diaper. And I gave up. I gave up the need to beat my house into organizational submission. The need to look amazing in every area of my life.

I embraced the grace in front of me, in the midst of all the unfinished, undone, and imperfect I found the One who is perfect. God was not concerned about my labeled living room toy baskets. He was concerned about my heart posture and my head perspective.

Did I trust in my pretty organization or in faith, hope, and love? Did I trust in myself to raise my children or in the King who created them? Did I trust in how others perceived me or how the King just loved me?

I needed strength to do some giving up. I needed strength to humble myself and wave the white flag. A strength that was beyond my own efforts, that released me from all the trying, and would propel me to trust God in the middle of my day. Could I trust God in the middle of big tantrums and hot anger at not being able to control a flippin' thing? In the middle of feeling like I was losing so much of me, my dreams, hopes, and strength?

Psalm 73:26 became a mantra: "My flesh and my heart may fail, but God is the strength of my heart and my portion forever."

I started to change diapers a little slower, with my chin a little higher, trusting in God's grace a little more. I chose to smile while diaper changing, and cereal feeding. Even when a tantrum threatened to steal my joy. I found grace in the yummy thigh rolls of my babies. I discovered grace in the middle of the night when I stopped counting the minutes, alone, nursing a sweet little one. I heard grace from friends who said they were with me in the mess of motherhood. I saw grace when a friend shrugged her shoulders at the clutter and continued to build train tracks on her carpet with her toddler.

I still felt ill-equipped in so many ways, but a few pieces were falling into place. A few truths. Some things felt a bit lighter.

God has grace for me, I started to say.

God is my strength, I whispered while nursing.

God is leading me, I coached my soul.

Things are bigger than myself, and for the first time in awhile, it felt good to be small. I found strength in weak places. It started to bring a bit of refreshment to know I wasn't dropped into motherhood and left to fail. When I became a mom, I was purposefully placed into a tender stream of grace. And when the stream of struggle seems to rise, God's grace rises higher. We are in a grace-stream that has been flowing since the beginning of time. Of Eden. Of salvation. Of mothering.

Chin up, dear Moms With Littles. The good news is getting grace doesn't require a road trip. Grace makes up for everything you lack. Everything you think you lack. And everything God knows you lack. Grace fills it in and calls it full, enough, and very good. The best news, grace can be found right in front of you, right in the middle of the diaper change you're about to do.

"Motherhood has a very humanizing effect. Everything gets reduced to essentials."

—Meryl Streep

2

Shift to See the Gift

Motherhood has a way of keeping our hearts low and humble. No one applauds us for doing puzzles, stacking blocks, and making forts. I don't particularly enjoy floor-life. Low and unnoticed. I like lights, cameras, and action. I lean toward brainstorming, strategizing, and creating spaces for those who long for God in our city. That kind of work gets me all kinds of excited and passionate...floor life, not so much.

Having fake conversations with topless Barbies just isn't my jam. Maybe it's yours, and if so, thanks be to God—grace comes easy to you on the floor. This girl is lifting her chin looking for grace all the time as I "play" Legos and find missing limbs for each tiny plastic Ninjago character.

After several years on the floor, I gave up. I called

in the grace hotline. I raised the white flag and admitted to myself, with tears streaming down my face, hiding in the bathroom: I am not enough on the floor. Such a simple thing to say, but an incredibly hard thing to surrender. To admit I don't enjoy being on the floor, I don't love pretend play, I don't like some parts of motherhood. The moment I came face to face with my abilities and realities of motherhood, a freedom flooded my mind and heart: I am not enough on the floor. But God's grace is. In fact, God's grace is enough for our entire motherhood.

His grace is enough, in what I love doing with my children and in what I don't. What I am good at and what I am not. What I can't wait to do and in what I dread.

There is a beautiful movement in our culture right now by Dr. Brené Brown about Wholehearted Living. One statement she encourages people to declare over themselves is "I am enough."

Her research wants to pull us out of a "scarcity culture"—where we wake up believing we don't have enough. She says the first thing we think when we wake up: "I didn't get enough sleep." And throughout the day we can have these thoughts:

"I don't have enough money."

"I don't have enough time"

"I am not enough."

I hear and feel all of this. Dr. Brown wants us to practice saying the opposite: "I am enough." But each time I said "I am enough" to myself, it felt hollow and flat.

I really wanted to believe I was enough.

But then I would lose my temper at my children, or I treated my husband like dirt, or jealousy crept into my heart about some other mom's situation, and it appeared like I was, once again, not enough.

So take your pick: my jealousy or my temper or my gossip or my lack of enthusiastically engaging small plastic people on the floor. I fall short. I don't live up to who I want to be. I am not enough.

I wasn't made to be "enough" on my own. Of course I would be frustrated and jealous. We are created to need God. Only God is "enough" to satisfy us, our souls, hearts, dreams, passions, and yes, even our mothering. Dr. Brené Brown is right, but she only gets us halfway there. We need to refocus our attention and shift our gaze off of lack and toward abundance, but our source can't be ourselves—it must be God.

I remember writing three words after Brené's "I am enough" statement in one of her books. I wrote each word slowly, as if the pause in my speed allowed the words to sink deep into my heart, anchoring with them the truth my soul longed for. "By God's grace."

I am enough...by God's grace.

God is enough.

God's grace is enough.

God's grace in me makes me enough.

By myself, I am certainly not enough.

The apostle Paul wrote about this very thing for us. In the middle of feeling at the end of himself, God spoke to him on this. Paul writes for us:

> *Because of the extravagance of those revelations, and so I wouldn't get a big head, I was given the gift of a handicap to keep me in constant touch with my limitations. Satan's angel did his best to get me down; what he in fact did was push me to my knees. No danger then of walking around high and mighty! At first I didn't think of it as a gift, and begged God to remove it. Three times I did that, and then he told me,*
>
> *My grace is enough; it's all you need.*
>
> *My strength comes into its own in your weakness.*
>
> *Once I heard that, I was glad to let it happen. I quit focusing on the handicap and began appreciating the gift. It was a case of Christ's strength moving in on my weakness. Now I take limitations in stride, and with good cheer, these limitations that cut me down to size—abuse, accidents, opposition,*

bad breaks. I just let Christ take over! And so the
weaker I get, the stronger I become.
—*2 Corinthians 12:7–10*

Paul has some kind of limitation given to him to keep him humble. We don't know what it was, but we know Paul did NOT see it as a gift. He begged God to remove his handicap.

Haven't we been there? Please God, make me better than this! Please God, take away my quick temper! Please God, remove my jealousy! I'm so thankful Paul was just like us. And after the third ask, God tells him a profound truth:

My grace is enough; it's all you need. My strength comes into its own in your weakness.

I always wondered how Paul heard this from God. A vision? Audible interaction? Paper airplane from heaven? Whatever the method, Paul lets the issue rest and even says he is cheerful about his limitations! He then just lets the handicap be what it was. Glad even, he says.

The next thing that happens is subtle, and if you're not looking, you might miss it. But let's not. Let's catch it and hang on. Paul says, "I quit focusing on the handicap and began appreciating the gift."

We watch Paul shift, to see the gift.

I can almost hear God saying, "Chin up, Paul. This

is actually a gift."

We have limitations, weaknesses, handicaps in our lives and specifically in our motherhood. And I have been there with Paul. Asking God to change something about myself so I could be better. Better at resting. Better at solitude. Better at gentleness. Better at boundaries. Especially better at motherhood.

What I needed to do was stop worrying about what I wasn't or didn't have, and focus on the gift God gave me. The gift of a weakness, so God's power is made perfect. So God's strength comes into its own. So I comprehend the fact that God's grace is all I need.

We push and pull, trying so hard to be perfect mothers. Many of us live in defeat, beating ourselves up, reluctant to receive His grace. Many of us live pretending to be perfect and find ourselves exhausted, again resisting grace. We might trust God's grace and goodness for our salvation, but somehow think motherhood is left up to us. Believing our motherhood hinges on our performance or ability brings us to the brink of anxiety, panic attacks, fear and depression. Grace is ours for the taking if we shift our perspective to see His gift.

Our fear of not being enough is a fear of rejection, a fear of shame, and a fear of failure. I don't know about you, but the "Rejection, Shame, Failure Cocktail" is not what I want to be drinking on a Saturday night. No thanks.

One of my fears is failure—screwing up my kids. So I work hard to make things just right, to discipline perfectly, and make good choices for my kids. Because motherhood really matters to us, failure in motherhood matters. When we fail at motherhood we hurt our very own children. The stakes are high, and we know it! We've all been hurt by our mothers and we don't seek to hurt our children.

The inevitable truth is this: we are going to mess up our children.

Dang it.

I cannot live motherhood perfectly. I have failed, I am failing, and I will fail. Find me a vat of ice cream. This is depressing.

I sat across from a counselor and friend for breakfast one early morning, seeking guidance in my life. He said it so casually I may have choked on my oatmeal. "You are going to mess up your children."

And he may have followed it with a question along the lines of, "Are you surprised that you are a human being?"

In the same bite of oatmeal, I discovered I was going to mess up my children and that I was delusional. I had really believed I was going to parent darn close to perfect. And save them from my mess. Who had I been kidding? Aside from myself!

Driving home from that eye-opening breakfast I had a choice. I could stay seated with the same view I've had for a while. Or I could shift to see the gift. The gift of weakness and brokenness.

I think I actually shifted in my seat as I drove. Making a physical move representing my soul adjustment.

I was given a gift of brokenness. I wasn't enough. It was time to grab for God's grace and realize that as a mother, I am not the hinge to health and happiness for my children. I am not the anchor. I am not the root for their growth.

Their Creator and King is. He made them, has a plan for their growth, with its valleys and mountaintops, and He is the Holy Hinge of their lives.

As sons and daughters who are now adults, we can look back and give grace to our parents because we can see they were doing the best they could. Or we are at least working toward extending grace. We can see their major mess-ups, downfalls, and limitations. The big picture comes into focus the farther away we get. We can also see the atmosphere they grew up in and the tools they had or lacked. As we extend grace, it brings freedom. Because grace holds no grudges.

We can see God poured grace all over our homes, and it dripped down over the mistakes of our parents. Many of us have endured hurtful words, hurtful situations, some even abuse, and we are still in the game.

We are here, with our chin up, in dignity. We are able to wear grace because it covers a multitude of sins. Because God's grace was poured out, we have breath in our lungs, and many of us are living vibrant lives.

Only by God's grace.

Let's get a little crazy and even take it one step further, and BOAST in our weaknesses, limitations, and handicaps in our motherhood because of how God's grace will use our downfalls for good. Which is insanity.

What Paul says right here is phenomenal. This is the same letter, said in a different way:

Therefore I will BOAST all the more gladly of my weaknesses, so that the power of Christ may rest upon me. For the sake of Christ, then, I am content with weaknesses, insults, hardships, persecutions, and calamities. For when I am weak, then I am strong.

—2 Corinthians 12:9–10

I can share with others how I don't love the Little Years and the floor-life, but God has helped me actually just love my children. I can boast in my limitations and His power that changes.

I can confess anger, sin, and yelling at my children, and boast in God's grace that covered it all. Grace steps in and fills in all my gaps. I can tell others about my failure and what I lack in motherhood, and watch the power of God rest on me.

Thank God. I want to move like Paul moved, who shifted to see the gifts of weakness.

When we shift our perspective and trust God and His grace, instead of hiding or perfecting ourselves, we actually begin to shift our entire LIFE. Our thinking changes, our heart changes, who we rely on changes. Motherhood was ever so slowly beginning to feel better on me, because God turns once-ragged garments into graceful gowns.

Chin up, God is enough in our motherhood.

"God invites us to come as we are, not to stay as we are."

—Timothy Keller

3

Maintaining and Sustaining

Laundry is the death of me. I want to DIE with each load. Like actual death. I am never getting it right. I put a load in and make a mental note to come back to change it, but I never do. I get busy with one hundred other mom things and I come back to a sour load. Like expired milk, only in a very large expensive container. I'm smelling it, looking at it, hoping it can somehow pass. How many times have I washed a load twice? As many as the stars in the heavens. Then the sorting. And folding. The actual putting it back in drawers. Laundry is an endless, cruel game. There is no winner. No one can ever just take their trophy and head on home.

This very idea of the constant, never-ending maintaining came up when I was reading material for a class I took at Regent Theological Seminary. "Everyday Spirituality" taught by professor Paul Stevens was a lifeline to me. I was a mile high in diapers, saturated in spit up, looking at laundry for days. My world was stains and bottles and sleep schedules. I was tired. Thirsty. Searching. I devoured this theology class.

What was I actually doing during my day? Was I doing anything significant? What did this all amount to? I had become the combination of a wet nurse and a maid. My brain resembled the inside of a toaster. Dry, useless crumbs leftover from a once delicious everything bagel. I was full of all the domestic things, but empty in the sense of home. I felt more at home when I was out with adults, having actual conversation, and donning mascara.

The first year with a baby was so many things. Things I had planned on and things I had never thought would challenge my soul. So I took a correspondence class with CDs of lectures and binders to read. As if I had the time. During nap times, I folded laundry to the sound of my professor's soothing voice. I squeezed in reading at bedtime and on weekends. I was thirsty for theology. For someone to lift my eyes above stacks of onesies and diapers, and above myself. God knew I needed to drink grace straight. No ice. Bottoms up.

The very first quote I read for my class was, "Not only is everyday experience no longer to be seen as an obstacle to being holy, but rather, it is to be understood as the primary forum for the journey toward holiness. Not only do we look at prayer as a space in which to become truly human, but we look at being truly human as the primary place of prayer."—Elizabeth Dryer

Everything within my sight was viewed as obstacles instead of opportunities. I wanted to get through the day in hopes I would be able to connect to adults, to God, to "real kingdom work" after my babies were sleeping. But these obstacles were my life. I had been wishing my life away, and bypassing so many gifts.

Professor Stevens showed us a series of ordinary pictures. Jogging shoes on the floor. An outdoor marketplace. A young woman on the Zambezi River canoeing. A broom in the corner of a kitchen. People playing chess. A child sleeping.

And he asked us: "Which picture most evoked a heart-hunger to know God in the midst of your life?"

Every single one of them. Could I know God in the middle of a diaper change? Was it humanly possible to know God while cleaning a toilet, playing on the floor, putting a child in time-out?

The Great I AM, who created and ordered the universe, maintains and sustains all of existence.

Colossians 1:17 says it succinctly: "He holds all things together."

My professor tenderly taught me everything in our ordinary lives was spiritual. Starting with the daily maintaining and sustaining we do. As image bearers of Christ, when we "maintain and sustain" the daily events in our microcosm of life, we reflect the image of God who maintains and sustains all life.

Never had I felt so much like God before in my entire life. Birthing, and now sustaining, my world of floundering, beautiful souls. It was the most fresh and familiar fact I had heard in months. Truth so tangible I could taste it.

Our everyday, ordinary, earthly lives mirror God's work. We need to know motherhood is deeply spiritual work.

We may not be soaring in our strengths as we fold laundry, but we are doing a God-activity called "Maintaining and Sustaining."

Just as God orders the stars, aligns the Earth on its axis, calms and brews the waves of the seas, and holds the breath of life in His hands, we as mothers have the opportunity to order our homes, families, and worlds. This is spiritually significant work! It may not feel glamorous after you've changed 30 dirty diapers, or done the seventh load of laundry in one day, but as we care for our people we allow them to see a glimpse of God.

We are entrusted with the blessing and gift of souls to raise. Psalm 127 likens children to "arrows in the hand of a warrior." If my children are called the arrows, then we are the warriors. We are warriors of the night, fighting fevers and protecting from monsters. We are warriors of the day, using Band-Aids as shields and hugs as hope. We are warriors of the heart, singing love over them and fortifying their spirits.

I felt my soul shift to see the gift. As if God was whispering, "Chin up, this is all kingdom work I've given you. Mothers are not second class. You are just like Me."

These amazing little souls have dignity, value, and worth. They are worth the mundane. They are worth the endless (kill me) laundry and lunch-packing and toilet-cleaning and homework helping and training and teaching. They are certainly worth the joys of our job: continual hugs, kisses, snuggles, smiling, holding, singing, playing, laughing, running, jumping, exploring, wondering.

The more this truth sank in, the more I wanted freedom for moms as they maintain and sustain. We need to liberate one another. This isn't just about me as a mom, it is about motherhood, fullstop. When you start to get a taste of grace in your life, you want to bring other people in on the goodness.

Let's give an extra measure of grace to the bathroom floor when the little boy can't make it in time to the toilet.

Let's extend grace for the unfolded laundry on the sofa.

Let's pass out grace for our living room splattered with Legos.

Sometimes we just need to pour out our messy selves on a trusted friend and find ourselves face to face with grace. Let's be grace-givers. Not just for our messy homes, but also for our messy hearts.

Let's keep one another accountable to the BEST kind of maintaining and sustaining. What is the best kind of maintenance? The kind that takes constant care of our children's hearts. Yes, we have domestic affairs to look after, but soul affairs matter more.

We find our bleacher voice all too easily for football games or soccer scrimmages. Let's do the same and cheer on the mom who maintains and sustains the very hearts of her children. Who spends time with her children. Who listens to their stories (foreeeeeever with the stories). Who leans in with love when she may just want to lie down in exhaustion. Who bends down to see them eye to eye, just like God.

We will cheer on the sacrifices of a mother, however they come. Whether it's laying down a job or picking one up. Whether it's letting a dream stay dormant for a season when a child requires much more than we planned. Whether it's setting aside sleep when the fever comes. When the nighttime fear sets in. When the teething arrives.

Let's cheer on the mom who points her child to the King; who tells them the stories of who Jesus is and what He taught and what He did. Especially then.

We have kingdom work right in our backyard.

We have kingdom work on the kitchen table.

We have kingdom work in the carpool line.

We have kingdom work in the doctor's office.

Kingdom work is all around us, as we raise our arrows to be strong and true. As we point them toward the King. As we, eventually, launch them into the world to change it by love.

Chin up, friend. Motherhood is both endless and eternal. Earthly and celestial. The divine found in the dirt.

*"You may forget that you are,
at every moment,
totally dependent upon God."*

—C.S. Lewis

4

The Spirituality of Motherhood

My "Everyday Spirituality" class brought such life and liberty to my bones. At the same time it brought death. A fantastic, necessary death. The death of the separation of spiritual activity and unspiritual activity. I had unknowingly put a divide between what was considered spiritual—ministry even—and what was not.

I had been working in college ministry for over 15 years. Meeting with sorority women and leading Bible discussions on campus and creating thirst for God in higher education. College men and women are such a blast—they are in the middle of adventure, decisions, and crisis. Simultaneously, for a continuous four years. I loved witnessing it. When I entered motherhood all action slowed to a crawl. The invigorating conversations I had savored were fewer, and my life zeroed in on my babies. I now had two loves: my children and my job as a campus minister. And I unknowingly put them in separate categories, "Amy the mom" and "Amy the Campus Missional Team Leader."

Rocking my baby boy, singing to him, pushing him in a stroller, feeding him, caring for him, cleaning his sheets, and washing his clothing felt so sweet in many ways. It was a privilege and a joy. It was something I had come to long for during a season of infertility. But at the very same time it felt incredibly mundane. Pedestrian. Ordinary.

Motherhood felt ordinary. Campus ministry felt spiritual.

Until Professor Stevens angled the camera in a different way. Correspondence classes can be so strange. I never met my professor, Paul Stevens. I just listened to him, read his work, emailed him, and wrote papers for him. But his impact was incredible. Thank goodness for satellite spiritual formation.

In *The Complete Book of Everyday Christianity* Robert Banks and Paul Stevens write, "The word 'ministry' is derived in both Greek and Hebrew from a word that simply means 'service.' A Christian servant is someone who puts himself or herself at God's disposal for the benefit of others and for the stewardship of God's world. Christian service—commonly called ministry—accords with God's purposes for people and the world and has the touch of God, often unknown to the servant. Christian service makes no distinction between the sacred and the secular. Washing dishes, designing a computer program, preaching a sermon, and healing the sick are all one, as William Tyndale said so long ago, 'as touching the deed to please God.' How far this is from contemporary thinking about ministry!"

I had unknowingly placed things done at church or church-like activity (college ministry) into a spiritual category. Pastoral care, preaching, evangelism—they were all in there. And all the rest were temporal, earthly, and of minor significance. I stored motherhood in the latter.

You may not feel tied to "spiritual" and "unspiritual" categories. But what about "significant" and "insignificant"? Does one part of your life feel significant and another feel less? Have you ranked things that feel "worth your time" and things that feel "boring and ordinary"?

Many of us live divided lives, and in our faulty thinking we divide our soul. We have anxiety about "being" when we think we ought to be "doing." Life on the floor is a simpler, slower, being-with-our-littles activity. Not much is "done." Life out in the world with decisions, board meetings, fast-paced deadlines, and lipstick and heels can give us checked boxes, praise, and a feeling of accomplishment.

But as my view shifted, so did my definitions. My categories. My entire life.

Stevens writes, "In the New Testament 'service' lasts and has significance to God not because of its religious character but because it is done in faith, hope, and love (1 Cor 3:9–15; 13:13 and 1 Thess 1:3). Sermons may dissolve in the fire of final judgment because they were preached for vain glory, while a sweater knit in love may be a ministry to Jesus (Matthew 25:40)."

Understanding this truth ripped the barrier of my separated soul. A sweater knit in love could have more meaning and significance than a sermon preached in vain? If I were honest, I would rank sermons higher than sweaters any day of the week. No matter the heart behind each piece of work.

I'm wired to think in categories. And suddenly there were none. My mind began reeling, but my soul began feeling. What used to be viewed as the boxes of "doing" and "being" now became transformed to "anything done in faith, hope, and love" and "anything NOT done in faith, hope, and love." This was a whole new refreshing world.

Stevens' thinking comes from Paul's first letter to

the Corinthian church. Paul talks about what kinds of things will last when it's all over. What will remain? What is eternal? Paul says anything done in faith, hope, and love will remain.

Diapers changed in love are pleasing to God and will somehow remain. Or I can change a diaper in bitterness. Bitterness at my life stage, my workload, my unmet expectations. Each moment is full of possible God-activity. Possible faith, hope, and love-activity. I could mop a floor in love. I could fold laundry in love. I could do a puzzle (save me) in love. No labeled box was big enough to contain what could be significant service to God!

What in the world will it look like as it lasts? Is each activity a sweet jewel added to the walls of the palaces in Heaven? Will each action done with a heart bent toward love be recounted as we walk and talk with the King when it's all over? I have no idea. But I like it. It frees me. This revelation was much messier than I thought, and I needed that.

He goes on, "In light of both Old and New Testament precedents, the following definition is proposed: Ministry (service) is any activity for which God is able to say, 'It is good' (Gen 1:31), and potentially involved a two-directional priestly service: touching people and places for God and touching God for people and places (whether or not it is known to the servant that

God is ministered to by his or her action (Mt 25:31–46)."—*The Complete Book of Everyday Spirituality*

My life became a level playing field. The significance of my day came from my heart, not my to-do list. I knew this on the edges, but it all came into focus for me. Probably because I was thirsty enough to go looking. To get my chin up. To quit naval-gazing and see what God had intended for us here on earth.

We can do almost anything in faith, hope, and love. All of my mothering can be done in love. And so much of it was. I was doing significant work. Spiritual work. Lovely, beautiful ministry.

We can drive to work, turn widgets, run board meetings, and teach classrooms out of faith, hope, and love. All things can be significant.

Likewise, I could do church work with selfish motives and an ugly heart. I could do it for self-promotion and applause. I could do it lacking so much faith, hope, and love.

Our heart posture is the hinge.

"The idea that the service to God should have only to do with a church altar, singing, reading, and the like is without doubt but the worst trick of the devil. How could the devil have led us more effectively astray than by the narrow conception that service to God takes place only in church and by works done therein...The whole world could abound with services to the Lord—not only in churches but also in the home, kitchen, workshop, field. (quoted in Feuchts, p. 80)"—*The Complete Book of Everyday Christianity*

Can you hear God's tender whisper? "Chin up, daughter. Your day can be as significant as you want, as spiritual as you'd like. Don't make it complicated. Don't be anxious. My burden is easy, my load is light."

And now these three remain: faith, hope, and love.
But the greatest of these is love.
—1 Corinthians 13:13

We give thanks to God always for all of you,
constantly mentioning you in our prayers,
remembering before our God and Father your work
of faith and labor of love and steadfastness of hope
in our Lord Jesus Christ."
—1 Thessalonians 1:3

"Letter writing is the only device for combining solitude with good company."

—Lord Byron

5

Four Things

While my children were in the "Little Years" I was learning, growing, failing, and gracing. Let's make grace a verb. The act of embracing grace on the regular. If I could have written myself a letter during that season it would have looked something like this:

Dear Self,

I know you only have a minute or two because things are CHAOTIC. You stink like spit-up, you haven't showered in days, and you're tired of smelling your sweats to see if you can get one more day out of them. You can, by the way. No one cares. "Let go and let God" on this one, dear.

You might resonate with some "Maybes."

Maybe you expected to sleep.

Maybe you expected your children would be calm and compliant.

Maybe YOU expected to be calm and collected.

Maybe you thought motherhood would be something it simply is not.

I stand with you in the Maybes. And so does God.

In fact, God does even more than stand next to us in our motherhood. He's got some real gifts for you. Remember what Isaiah says about God and mothers:

Go on up to a high mountain,
O Zion, herald of good news;
lift up your voice with strength,
O Jerusalem, herald of good news;
lift it up, fear not;
say to the cities of Judah,
"Behold your God!"
Behold, the Lord God comes with might,
and his arm rules for him;
behold, his reward is with him,
and his recompense before him.
He will feed his flock like a shepherd;
he will carry the lambs in his arms;
he will hold you close to His heart,
and gently lead those that are with young ones.
—Isaiah 40:10–11

First of all, there is a lot of "go up to a high mountain" and "lifting up your voice" language. There is a clear shift in thinking. You are called to think higher thoughts and to look above your rising waters of sleep deprivation. You are coached to keep your chin up. You need a different view of who you are and who God is. You have made your laundry too big and your King too small. With all due respect, you've elevated yourself too high in your thinking and have placed a mighty God too low in your mind. God comes in might. He comes with a ruling arm. His reward is with Him. This is no small god.

Check out the last four verses. That part is jampacked with good things. And it's just for moms. Just for you.

God does four beautiful things for those who are with young ones. Which is you, sister! Bingo. You qualify. So lean your tired bones toward the truth and listen:

God feeds you.

Don't you need some nourishment, as you feed your babies?

God carries you.

Don't you need to be carried, as you carry your littles around?

God holds you close to His heart.

Don't you need to be held close to God's chest, as

your Little sleeps on yours?

God gently leads you.

Don't you need to be gently led, cared for, and loved as you pour out your energy and your life for others?

Yes. Yes you do. Thank God. He wants to do these things for you. Tell Him you want Him to do that. Let Him. Take a deep breath and whisper a few words to Him.

Soak in these truths today. Let them surround you like a warm bath that heals your brokenness and bitterness. Let God's leadership and gentleness be your strength today. Go back and read that whole passage again. You have time. You have one more minute to spare here.

He feeds, carries, holds, and gently leads. What a tenderhearted grace He has for mothers. For you. Don't be fooled by whatever else you are hearing. By what some may be telling you about God. The King is good, powerful, and gentle. He is worthy of our highest praise, and He has come to our lowest valley.

Take one of those four grounding words, each morning this week, and let it wash over your unmet expectations and your frustrations.

Let it soften you and strengthen you.

Let it nourish you.

Chin up, sister. God is FOR you and He is WITH

you. Feeding, carrying, holding, and gently leading you.

Maybe yesterday's makeup, unfolded onesies, and sour burp cloths will pale in comparison to the fact that God is for you.

Maybe closing your eyes and imagining Him carrying you will relieve some stress and give you comfort.

Maybe letting yourself listen for God—letting yourself be led by Him—will refresh your soul.

If you take a minute to lift up your thoughts about Him, these Maybes will turn to Yeses. He will not only shift your perspective, He will shift your very life. You will see things from His view and you will find grounding grace-gifts everywhere.

Affectionately,
Your Few-Steps-Ahead-Self

"We are a nation of exhausted and overstressed adults raising over scheduled children. We use our spare time to desperately search for joy and meaning in our lives. If we want to live a whole hearted life, we have to be very intentional about cultivating sleep and play, and about letting go of exhaustion as a status symbol and productivity as self worth."

—Brené Brown

"Liberty, when it begins to take root, is a plant of rapid growth."

—George Washington

6

Growing Oaks

I had some new pegs to hang my thoughts on about the spirituality of motherhood, now I had to actually practice living this way. It's one thing to read it, it's another thing to do it. I wanted to practice accomplishing nothing for periods of time. To practice being present and enjoying my sweet kids.

But it feels so risky to commit to accomplishing nothing before noon. It seems scary. What will I show for my day? What will happen to the laundry? Can I stand to see the crumbs under the table and NOT vacuum them? Can I trust Jesus with a morning of forts, reading, coloring, and child-directed play? For several hours strung together?

While these questions swirled in my mind, I was sensing my middle child was crying out in every way for attention. I had taken her to the pool, invited friends over to play, and read to her in between my house chores, emails, and to-do's. Yet she needed more right now. Her five-year-old heart was having a growth spurt that needed MY love to ground it and root it so she could grow straight and strong. Not crooked and calloused.

But I resisted.

Because life on the floor is unproductive. And letting things go for a while would put me behind.

Behind.

Behind what? Behind whom? Behind some invisible line of impossible? Behind the mom I was supposed to be? Behind a false sense of order? Behind empty promises of organized everything? Or behind a polished self, hiding my actual self?

When was the last time I challenged my son to a ping pong game? Weeks. What kept me from playing with my son?

Feeling behind. It seems I may need to rethink my timeline. My expectations. My place in line. I may need to rethink the line itself. I'd created an impossible line and set the bar too high even for myself. It was time to sideline my impossible standards.

It was mid-summer in Ohio. Soaked, glimmering grass was left from last evening's downpour, towels left hung to dry were now dripping. The house was quiet. My coffee was perfect. Sunshine poured through the back room, light and lovely. The day was presenting itself before me. Another summer day home with all three of my children. And I had just agreed with God to slow it all down. Emotional tanks were looking half-filled, and ironically the one thing we needed was nothing.

So I set out to let the kids decide for a few hours what we would or would not do. I had suggestions, but I also had a fierce commitment to "Nothing To Show Until After Noon." A commitment to "being" and not "doing." To seeing my children. To knowing them more. To loving them well.

We stayed in our pj's. Stayed on the couch. Stayed free and untethered. Unattached to time, agenda, or accomplishment. It all sounds cozy and comfortable, but it was just the opposite. Uncomfortable. Like a very hard thing before me. Like a discipline. Like holding back the flood of "Let's go to the Library! Let's go to the park! Let's get dressed and out the door and DO SOMETHING!"

So we stayed lazy. We read books. We snuggled. We built car ramps, and the three-year-old, the-five-year-old and the ten-year-old all created car contests and race tracks. Together. I am still shocked writing that. I think it had something to do with not needing to be anywhere or accomplish anything. Something to do with a slower momma. Something to do with grace.

We did puzzles and I did some deep breathing try-ing to fit pieces into place. Puzzles could easily be the end of me. If given the option: would you like to sta-ple two fingers to one another or do a puzzle? It'd be a tough call. My greatest sanctification and growth comes from puzzles. They are a spiritual discipline.

We were on the floor much of the morning. My StrengthsFinder results will tell you that life on the floor may be a very awkward fit. Like a dress that looked sideways and frumpy on me. Four out of the five of my strengths are in the Influencing category. And the world's definition of influence is usually on some kind of stage, with some kind of voice, and some kind of vision.

And I had forgotten. I had forgotten that my people need my influence. These are God's creations in my home. Budding disciples under my roof. And what does Jesus do with His people, His disciples? He gets low. He serves them. He washes their feet. He gives them intentional, undivided attention. He influ-ences their entire lives with His love.

These three little souls are my stage, my voice, my vision. These children are the lives I will influence the most. It won't be by dragging them around, it won't be by hurry. It won't be by wishing them older.

It won't be by yelling. It won't be by pulling and shoving and running ragged in and out of car seats and in and out of peace.

It will be by love. By servant-leadership. By getting low and getting grateful. It will be in the humble moments, kneeling with cars and dolls and hunching over to squeeze into toddler-size forts. It will be more quiet and more honest and more slow. Just the way a solid oak would grow. With a quiet strength, day by day. Which is exactly what God calls us to grow up into. And we don't have to strain to produce the beauty of lovely, leafy branches. It's Jesus Himself that grows us up. Jesus, when He first started His ministry, kicked it off in the temple by standing up and reading these words written hundreds of years before:

The Spirit of the Lord God is upon me,
because the Lord has anointed me
to bring good news to the poor;
he has sent me to bind up the brokenhearted,
to proclaim liberty to the captives,
and the opening of the prison to those who are bound;
to proclaim the year of the Lord's favor,
and the day of vengeance of our God;
to comfort all who mourn;
to grant to those who mourn in Zion—

to give them a beautiful headdress instead of ashes,
the oil of gladness instead of mourning,
the garment of praise instead of a faint spirit;
that they may be called oaks of righteousness,
the planting of the Lord, that he may be glorified.
They shall build up the ancient ruins;
they shall raise up the former devastations;
they shall repair the ruined cities,
the devastations of many generations.
—Isaiah 61:1-4

Jesus has come for us. And He comes bringing good news, binding up broken hearts, liberating captives, and opening up our prisons. He comes with a crown of beauty instead of ashes, and gladness instead of mourning. So we who follow Him will be called Righteous Oaks. Planted by God Himself. For His glory.

From the beginning, we see God getting down in the dirt. He was creating, making, perhaps hand-planting some parts of the earth. Planting His creation with His voice and His heart. We see Him plant us here. So we can grow up and do great things like build up ancient ruins, raise up formerly devastated places, and repair ruined cities.

He is raising us up to raise up others.

And He does it all in love. It was love alone that

compelled Him to lay down his very life.

God waters us with love. He grows and sustains us with love. He uses the elements to make us strong with His love. We are growing into strong oaks and have been since we were little seedlings.

By this same love, we can work with God and together grow our babies up strong and tall. Into oaks of righteousness. The plantings of the Lord.

Chin up, Momma. Growing beautiful, strong, and dignified oaks takes grace, truth, and time.

"My brokenness is a better bridge than my pretend wholeness ever was."

—Sheila Walsh

7

Step Outside

A few days after my extended floor commitment, I found myself at my favorite coffee shop sitting on one side of an outdoor table with a light summer breeze at my back. The morning sun was just enough and the coffee was hand-pressed. Summer was singing her song of freedom. Opposite me sat a young, beautiful, defeated mom. I could see the edges of her free spirit, but exhaustion had eclipsed most of it. She shared her story; she had been breaking for a while. Reaching for help and hope, she opened up her life and showed the cracks. She sat broken and beautiful in front of me and asked, "How do you have any time for your dreams as a mom?" Depression, anger, and failure at our own impossible standards were our topics that morning in our safe and solitary seats. We talked about watching dreams dry up. We named our tears and unmet expectations. Life can feel so bleak and colorless when our kids are so little.

With full truth and abundant grace I was able to say life with littles is for just a little while. And that for those of us who dream and find ourselves in a holding tank in the Little Years—it is not for naught. God is growing everyone from the floor up. Oak-strength is happening.

I had to strengthen my soul on the floor, before my spirit would be able to fly.

God has some watering, sunning, and pruning to do in our lives. However, much of it happens at ground level. On the floor. Humble and low, as we love our sweet little ones. As they grow up, so do we. So do the possibilities. So do the opportunities. So does the space and time to try our dreams. To write. To sing. To play. To fuel a dormant dream.

It's a different season to have two of my three in school all day. A season changed when we were done changing diapers. My brain showed up again just when I thought I had lost my ever-loving mind.

Diapers, late nights, early mornings, breakfast, lunch, dinner, repeat—this is the grit where we find God. The grime that God uses for growth. I have to lean into God's grace, trusting He will make up for all the gaps I have left.

This young mom asked about this, too: "How do you do that? I find it a nice concept, but I don't know how to find God and His help when I am about to explode at my kids. When I am wiping bottoms. I ask Him for help in those moments and He's not there." Desperate for the practical hand of God in her motherhood, she asked honestly. She wanted to understand.

So I pointed to the outside job that brings inside peace. It seems that if I don't do the work of sorting through my unmet expectations, sifting out the lies I believe, and retraining my brain with truth outside of the gritty motherhood moments, then I won't be able to shift my perspective inside those moments. If I don't get healthy away from my people, then I can't be healthy with my people. If I step outside of it all and get hope, I can step inside of it all and give love.

Maybe it's counseling.

Where you get out of your home and get some perspective. So you can transfer that better perspective to the bedtime battle and the "Get Your Shoes On" struggle.

Maybe it's medicine.

Where you get your serotonin going again. So you can get out of bed and see you are stronger than your strong-willed toddler.

Maybe it's meeting with a friend who has walked this road before.

Where she prays with you, reads truth with you, and tells you Jesus was perfect so you don't have to be. And you take the grace with you when you fail at being perfect; when you raise your voice at your child again when you swore you wouldn't. You take grace and whisper to your soul, long after you've apologized to your child, "I am forgiven. Thank you God, for pouring grace on even this."

Maybe it's finding a Bible and looking at Jesus, with no children around.

Like, actually pausing all of your previous thoughts about Him and consider afresh what He teaches, how He treats others, and who He is. Turn to John chapter 8, and brace yourself. Watch the woman, the crowd, and the Pharisees and see how you painfully relate to each one. Then shift your focus to center stage and watch Jesus. He looks at this woman and sees, quite clearly, all of her shame. He understands her shame. He knows her shame. Then He does the unthinkable. He shields her shame. His response writes love over her shame. And from this one conversation, He shifted this woman's entire life.

When we get outside of our situation, when we shift to see the gifts, God's gifts will change our lives. We find we don't have to hide our shame or perfect our lives. Instead, we accept that Jesus wrote Love over Shame and we have stepped out of the world's stream for our motherhood. We now confidently stand in the gentle stream of grace.

This sweet mom in front of me was doing this outside work, so she would work well on the inside. Sitting with an older mom, pouring out her heart, seeking wisdom and help. She was taking notes and soaking in my mistakes. Apart from her children, adult to adult. Apart from sticky hands, sour attitudes, and slimy walls. She was growing like an oak right in front of me. She was a beautiful and broken tree. Being pruned and tended. Her heart was having a growth spurt that needed God's love to ground it and root it, so she could grow straight and strong. Not crooked and calloused.

Friend, step outside. Get out of your house. Out of your routine. Out of your head.

And look at it all from a removed place. Write what you see, what you like, what you don't. And make a plan to change your view. Make a plan to find a counselor, find a friend, find a new way of thinking. The Psalms are a great place to start.

I have come to resonate so often with the poet who writes:

I lift up my eyes to the mountains—
where does my help come from?
My help comes from the Lord,

the Maker of heaven and earth.
He will not let your foot slip—
he who watches over you will not slumber;
indeed, he who watches over Israel
will neither slumber nor sleep.
The Lord watches over you—
the Lord is your shade at your right hand;
the sun will not harm you by day,
nor the moon by night.
The Lord will keep you from all harm—
he will watch over your life;
the Lord will watch over your coming and going
both now and forevermore.
—Psalm 121

The poet starts right where we can start: lifting his eyes up. He gets his chin up. He searches for help. We can be scrubbing dishes, filling out permission slips, running errands, or coming from work, and we can simply lift up the eyes of our heart. And remember that help is here. Help is here from the most powerful source of all—the Maker of heaven and earth. He hasn't fallen asleep on us. He's watching over us, keeping us, shading us.

And we can softly whisper some truths:

"God I am so tired, but you never tire. I'm thankful you don't sleep so I can."

"God don't let my foot slip. Your word says you won't. I am trusting You."

"God, you are watching over me. Thank you."

"God, you are my help. I need You."

"God, you are the keeper of my whole day. Be near right now."

"God, shade me from lies. Keep me in truth."

I am lifting up eyes with you, sister, gaining perspective outside of my little world. Outside my tiny view on God. And finding help, hope, healing.

Chin up, friend. God sees you. God knows you. God keeps you.

"Never lose an opportunity of seeing anything beautiful, for beauty is God's handwriting."

—Ralph Waldo Emerson

8

Beauty Instead of Ashes

It was a cool, late May morning, around 7 a.m. My eyes still shut as I was slowly waking to the world. The heat of the sun streaming through the curtain. My mind failed to process my watermelon sized belly as I attempted to turn on my side. Oh, yeah. I was big-pregnant. Moving around was a chore. Getting up was an actual workout. I needed a forklift to move me to the bathroom.

Edging out of bed, my big 34 week pregnant self felt off. Not just third trimester uncomfortable. My brain triggered a warning that something was not quite right. Suddenly it dawned on me what was happening. Things were really, really wet down there. "Great," I thought. "I have six weeks to go and I am losing bladder control now. This is how it's gonna be.

Awesome. Don't mind me. I'll be wetting the bed each morning, folks."

Turns out, I didn't lose bladder control, my water broke and my baby was on his way. As quickly as my water broke, I realized so did my expectations. Puddling on the floor were all my hopes of my birth story. This puddle was my actual narrative. Everything was happening all too soon. He wasn't supposed to come until July. He needed to cook longer. He couldn't come out yet. Why was this happening? What did this mean? What were we supposed to do?

We arrived at the hospital, and the nurse in triage said, "Hmmmm…as I am looking at your charts…this better not be your water breaking. You still have six more weeks."

This better not be my water breaking? Seriously? That's the hope you're going to offer me right now?

WELL WHAT IF IT IS, LADY?

And it was.

My firstborn son was born six weeks early. He wasn't your typical preemie—he came in at 5 lbs 10 ounces. But he was "flaccid" as his lungs were slightly underdeveloped and he needed help breathing.

So we spent 23 days in the NICU.

Motherhood was supposed to start off with beauty and peace. Not chaos and confusion. I did not expect to learn how to nurse with bright hospital lights and sixteen other babies all around me and a very small folding screen for my "privacy." All my dreams of low-lit, quiet, serene nursing images went out the window. I expected to take my baby home, like a regular person, after a few days of healing and being cared for by nurses. I expected all my friends to pass my baby around and "oohhh" and "ahhh." But when your baby is connected to tubes and has "limited stimulation" this proves to be just the opposite. This was just the beginning of my unmet expectations of motherhood. From my first birth until now, I am continually shedding my unmet expectations.

What are the unmet expectations in your motherhood? What did you think motherhood would be, but is not?

Did you expect one baby and got two?

Did you expect to sleep train and have a non-sleeper?

Did you expect to parent as a couple and find yourself a single mother?

Did you expect to love motherhood and find yourself overwhelmed or frustrated?

I once heard Jen Hatmaker say, "We need to let go of what we expected and embrace what we have." Once we acknowledge our unmet expectations, we can honestly assess our gifts. The gifts in front of us, not just the ones we wish we had. What gifts of motherhood are in front of you?

I want to encourage you to make an old-fashioned list. You know the kind. Find actual paper and real ink and give it a go. Label your first list: "Ashes of Unmet Expectations," and write down all you thought you would have or experience. Maybe your "Ashes of Unmet Expectations" includes getting sleep, feeling in control, working more, having free time, or enjoying puzzles on the floor...

Then make a list right next to it, calling it: "Crowns of Beauty." Name all the gifts you actually have.

Your list of "Crowns of Beauty" could include your child's wonder, snuggles and giggles, your child's adventurous spirit, sweet little toes, the best laughter you'll ever hear, hilarious storytelling, or outrageous statements...

Chin up, friend. See what you find.

When I sit down and make the effort to shift to see the gifts, things clear up. It's clear God wants to take our unmet expectations—those ashes that are killing us daily—and make them crowns of beauty. That's what He loves to do. He came to bind up our broken hearts. He came to take our mourning and our grief and our ashes. He came, instead, to give us crowns of beauty.

So we come back to Isaiah again. To the chapter that grows us up into oaks of righteousness. This time we look at it from a different view point. This time we see comfort for those who mourn, and ashes that turn into beauty:

The Spirit of the Lord God is upon me...
he has sent me to bind up the brokenhearted,
to proclaim liberty to the captives,
and the opening of the prison to those who are bound...
to comfort all who mourn;
to grant to those who mourn in Zion—
to give them a crown of beauty instead of ashes,
the oil of gladness instead of mourning,
the garment of praise instead of a faint spirit;
that they may be called oaks of righteousness,
the planting of the Lord, that he may be glorified.
They shall build up the ancient ruins;
they shall raise up the former devastations;
they shall repair the ruined cities,
the devastations of many generations.
—Isaiah 61:1–4

Do you see those "Insteads" in there? A crown of beauty instead of ashes, oil of gladness instead of mourning? Our King is all about redemption, grace, and restoration. Those are His gifts to us. He loves a good "Instead." A barrel of wine instead of water. A healed daughter instead of sickness. An empty grave instead of death.

I grappled with my unmet expectations. I remember holding Robby in the NICU, crying and wrestling with my birth story, as I thought, "How do I accept these bright lights and cranky nurses? How do I nourish a baby who can't suck, struggles to swallow, and isn't breathing on his own? How do I accept this mess is my motherhood?"

How do I accept that this is my motherhood with my hot tears and my jealousy and my aching, bleeding body? Then Paul's words rang in my ear, "My grace is sufficient for you, for My power is made perfect in your weakness." This was my weakness. Motherhood had become my weakness. I had expected it to be my strength.

I didn't get a cape with motherhood. I got weakness. And then I got grace.

With a busted up body, a struggling baby, and an unfamiliar place, I was certainly not enough. Here, in the weakness of my motherhood, is where God's power was made perfect in me.

It was His power that steadied my hand as I pulled Robby off of me so he could take in air as he nursed. His power was present while all the alarms went off, as he lost oxygen levels, and as nurses came and we watched our baby choke on milk and fight for air.

It was terrifying. Yet, I had strength in the terrifying moments. In the weak places. In the what-in-the-world-am-I-doing-and-why-am-I-allowed-to-be-a-mom places. By God's grace we endured, and we learned to thrive, not in the power we possessed, but in the power He granted through weakness. We found love instead of fear.

There is so much room for ashes in motherhood. For grief. For mourning. And I have found there is just as much—possibly even more—room for beauty here, too. Humility connects us to the beauty in motherhood. When we wave our white flag and say we are not enough, we open up a world of beauty. Motherhood is one of the most humbling and beautiful gifts we've been given.

If we continue to speak our needs, admit our failures, and shed our perfectionism, God has gifts for us. We will have praise instead of a faint spirit. Laughter instead of mourning. Joy instead of sorrow.

When we embrace our limitations and humble ourselves toward God, He gives us grace. Remember what James says to us: "But He gives a greater grace. Therefore it says, 'God is opposed to the proud, but gives grace to the humble.'"—James 4:6

If we humbly say, "I did not expect a child like this"...then there is grace to embrace the gift of who our child is. We can begin to see the crowns of beauty around us.

If we humbly say, "I did not expect motherhood

to be SO crazy, hard, and exhausting"...then we can receive the grace to embrace the gift of what we actually have.

If we humbly say, "I cannot do it all"...then we can open our hearts to receive the power of God's strength, and it is exactly what is enough.

My Ashes List, throughout the years, has sometimes been long, sometimes short. Right now it's looking like:

I expected to be patient.

I expected to not care about the mess in the middle of creativity.

I expected to enjoy life on the floor.

I expected to love my children perfectly.

I expected to be perfect.

My Beauty List usually ends up longer than my Ashes List. I have watched my heart swell, and the ink flow with thankfulness the longer I lift my chin up. The more I shift to see the gifts.

I have a healthy, smart, witty, ten-year-old boy with no residual prematurity issues.

I have a creative daughter with a leader's heart and the best imagination.

I have a take-the-bull-by-the-horns three-year-old-

boy as my youngest, wild one.

I have children with bright minds and bright futures.

I have joy when I hold them and sing to them.

I have hope when I hear them sharing, hear them laughing, hear them being friends.

I have thankfulness they are mine to raise, with their sweet, curious eyes.

I have laughter in the wiffle ball games, and pride in my children swinging bats and trying new, hard things.

I have tears of joy when I see them loving foster children, when I see them share their toys.

I have a brimming home of crazy characters.

I have my chin up, just a bit higher, seeing God in the middle of the mundane, in the middle of madness.

Chin up. God loves to give us beauty instead of ashes.

"Did I offer peace today? Did I bring a smile to someone's face? Did I say words of healing? Did I let go of my anger and resentment? Did I forgive? Did I love? These are the real questions. I must trust that the little bit of love that I sow now will bear many fruits, here in this world and the life to come."

—Henri Nouwen

"For every minute you remain angry, you give up sixty seconds of peace of mind."

—Ralph Waldo Emerson

9

On Anger and Acorns

Early on in our marriage, my husband came home one frigid January evening to find our "sound system" (think 1990's boombox) laying face down in the white, freshly fallen snow. Puzzled, he came in the back door from a long day of work to hear his steaming wife snarl: "It doesn't work, so it belongs out with the trash." He tilted his head and started to ask some calm, clarifying questions.

A few hours before he had gotten home I had hoped to play music in the house. A reasonable request. What became unreasonable was how LONG it took me to get the thing working. Wires had become loose on the boom box, it was going on ten years old, and I was growing increasingly impatient. So I snapped. Like, crazy-lady stuff. I picked up that boom box, kicked open the back screen door, struggled to hold it open while I pried apart the heavy apartment door, and flung it high up into the unsuspecting snowflakes. My husband's surprise 16th birthday present landed face first in the snow. Bereft of love and tenderness. Alone and left to freeze to death. I could not care less.

Now mind you, the man I married is as calm as the day is long. We are going on seventeen years of marriage, and I have never heard him even raise his voice. I know, right now you are questioning my honesty. But it's true. He is strong, steady, and silent in the face of crazy. Praise the Good Lord, because crazy is what he married.

Me? I grew up where yelling, cursing, and road rage were just part of life. Add my genetics to my own saucy personality, and well, let's just say it's a whole new level of anger.

My dad's hot temper was mostly geared toward inanimate objects (i.e. toilets) and fixing things. If a wrench, hammer, or general plumbing was involved, you had a sudden desire to play outside. To be quite fair, I saw that same anger defend a daughter who had gotten pushed down on her rollerblades by an older bully. The offender was picked up, firmly placed against a wall, and warned to never push anyone like that again. Anger in defense of the powerless is anger we can all get behind.

However, my own anger was directed at my sweet children. When I became a mom, my unmet expectations collided head on with my children and the result? Yelling. I hated it. I couldn't believe how I could quickly transform from staying calm and redirecting a toddler one minute, and the next I was yelling at them for not listening and getting their shoes on NOW. Getting out the door (transitions), mealtime, and bedtime were my hotspots.

I came across this proverb early one morning in some of my more angry days and I sat stunned:

Whoever has no rule over her own spirit is like a
city broken down, without walls.
—Proverbs 25:28

Broken. Down. Those two words stared into my soul. I was both broken and down and my chin was entirely too heavy to get up. It took all my strength to reach out to my counselor again for help and hope. He was outside my life, my little family, and my head. I needed someone on higher, sturdier ground to reach down and help me out of my hole.

My counselor was always shocking me with statements I had never heard before. He graciously said, "Losing control is never an option."

Never?

Wow. I thought it was. And of course, it is an option, but not a healthy one. In my world, losing control meant yelling, and yelling did several unhealthy things to my children and spouse.

I learned raising our voices actually freezes the part of the brain that learns. Yelling does not open learning, it actually shuts it down. In that moment, our children are not being trained in the way they should go because they are frozen. They cannot think well, their little brains are scrambled, and they are afraid. My counselor talked about how, at a very basic assessment, many men and women in prison grew up being yelled at (among other things); they often cannot think well or make good choices because of it.

Broken. Down. Shocked. Helpless. My list was growing longer and heavier. My motherhood dress was revealing ugly parts and no matter how much I adjusted it, my anger was showing. Maybe you have grabbed your child too hard, criticized, name-called, or withdrawn from your children. Either way, you felt like your dress was tucked into your panties, and it simply was not pretty. Yelling was the most-used tool in my back pocket. Yet it was a tool I always hated using. I longed to bury it and use something else. Something needed to shift.

We discussed a variety of tools, one of them being

anti-anxiety medicine or antidepressants to calm the crazy enough so I could respond well. My knee-jerk reaction to meds was a firm, "No." Give me all the other tools first, please. The Christian world can be a crazy place, and for a variety of ungrounded reasons, meds felt opposite to faith. But this is where I interrupt my own narrative, with hindsight, and have some real talk with you, dear friend: Jesus gave us Tylenol, casts, doctors, hospitals, surgeons, medicine, oils, good healing foods, and our brains. We live in a fallen, broken world. When things broke in the garden of Eden, everything broke. Our relationships broke, the Earth broke, and our bodies broke. Sometimes we need an emergency C-section. Sometimes our arms need casts. Sometimes our brains lack serotonin. Meds are not opposite of faith. Sometimes it takes great faith to take meds. We'll chat more on this soon.

But I didn't have ears to hear this or eyes to see it, so I went with some other, still very necessary tools. I appealed to my strength of competition and started training. I had not seriously worked on keeping myself under control, especially when the heat rises.

If losing control was never an option, then it was time to do some mental weightlifting. What were my tools when my temperature rose, my breath got heavy, and rage rounded the corner? We made a list: I can walk away. Go into the bathroom for a mom time-out. Blow out an imaginary candle. Count to 10. Replace anger with empathy. I can state the number I am at between 1–10 on the anger scale so my husband knows I need a break. He has come home a few times and I have said, "I'm at a 9." He often responds, "Go take a walk. I've got it." I can have a pocketful of consequences for my children, prepped and ready to say calmly.

The city walls of my soul had been broken down for too long. It needed fortification. Yes, I needed to practice self-control. But not on my own power. I had to start my day low, with my chin looking up. My practice started with a humble and honest heart before God each morning. Confessing my weakness and lack of self-control. Asking Him to fill me with the power of His Spirit. Inviting Him to reveal what was beneath all the anger.

Jesus gives us not only medicine but books too. Medicinal books. I dug into a healing book titled *Controlling Anger Before It Controls You* by Gregory Jantz. I know, sounds like a really good beach read. Except not.

He has sections like "The Root of Anger," "The Branches of Anger," and "Uprooting and Pruning the Roots and Branches."

What I found: Guilt, shame, and fear are big factors. So is stress, keeping a record of wrongs, and unmet expectations. And in the "Unmet Expectations" chapter, he takes us to none other than Chicken Little. Never has a children's story been so mind-blowing:

> Do you remember the children's story of Chicken Little? She goes out for a stroll one day and winds up walking under a tree and being hit in the head by a falling acorn. Immediately, Chicken Little decides 'The sky is falling! The sky is falling!' She proceeds to act under that perception, gathering up several of her friends to go to the king about this crisis. In the heat of the moment, Chicken Little and her friends are tricked and ultimately eaten by a clever fox they meet on the way to the king.

> Chicken Little walked straight under the branch of Unrealistic Expectations. When the acorn hit her head, she took it as a catastrophe. It wasn't a catastrophe; it was a natural event. Acorns fall from trees. She just happened to be hit by one. She could have said, 'Ouch! I just got hit by a falling acorn!' and continued on with her walk. Instead, that acorn became 'The sky is falling!'

> I wonder how many times this happens for women. Unrealistic expectations turn the acorns of problems, shortcomings, hiccups, and bumps in the road into catastrophes. Problems,

shortcomings, hiccups, and bumps in the road are not special to you; they are a part of the human condition."—Gregory Jantz

Dang it.

I had turned acorns into astronomical problems, expected life to feel a certain way, and hoped transitions, mealtimes, and bedtimes would just run themselves. If my expectations failed, then I got angry.

I was in a cycle of falling sky pieces and stress and negativity and anger. I wanted off the hamster wheel.

Acceptance is key to shifting our expectations. We live in a messy broken world. Acorns fall off trees. It's a natural occurrence. No one is exempt, so why would I think I am?

Around this same time, a friend shared that he uses a word to help him properly place hiccups in his day in context. If he forgets something or does something stupid or misplaces something, he says, "Bummer."

No beating ourselves up.

No beating others up.

That's a bummer, that's an acorn, and we will be ok.

So I practiced saying, "What a bummer you can't find your shoes. Look again. I'll wait." Normally, I would have started to shame and blame them in anger about their misplaced shoes and huffed around trying to find them myself.

I practiced getting down and face to face with them, listening with empathy, when they came to me sad about all kinds of sad kid-things. Left to myself, I would have stood over them and wanted them to suck it up and deal.

I practiced knowing my trigger spots and building in time to not rush us out the door, to train our children to stay at the table while eating, to listen to their questions and stories that tumble out when they are laying in bed thinking about their day. Ordinarily I would have been frustrated by all the time each of these activities took. But these aren't activities. These are the lives of my children.

I had forgotten my number one job was to train up a child in the way she should go. This is not a side project in my life; motherhood is not a nuisance. Motherhood is full-time (no matter what other job you may have) and an honor. Slowing down and taking the time to help my children accept responsibility and embrace integrity is a fantastic use of my time. Getting out the door in love instead of anger, eating meals with laughter instead of tears, and giving baths with plenty of time instead of rushing them into pj's and kisses and good nights is all part of the gift of motherhood.

Motherhood became two-way training. I needed to be trained up as a mom at the very same time I was training up my children. I was broken down, but I was watching God build my walls back up. I remembered Isaiah 61 once again, and this time, the last part of the section spoke to me:

> *They shall build up the ancient ruins;*
> *they shall raise up the former devastations;*
> *they shall repair the ruined cities,*
> *the devastations of many generations.*

Do you see this? She who has no rule over her own spirit is like a city broken down, without walls. But God grows us up in order to repair the ruined cities, the generational faults, and the broken down walls. And faith, hope, and love are our tools of the trade. We can call an acorn what it is and keep the sky in its proper place. We can practice seeing bumps in the road and waves that crash all day long as part of the human experience. We can see ourselves as belonging to one another and not set apart in our shortcomings and hiccups. We can accept that there are bummers all around, and we can acknowledge it all and keep going.

Chin up, friend. God is the Repairer of City Walls.

"We are learning to make space for two callings in one home, in one marriage."

—Shauna Niequist

10

Two Callings, One Roof

During our first October with the same last name, my husband and I were having conversations about our jobs and our dreams and our hopes. He looked at me and said: "I am more sure of your calling than mine... so let's figure out how to get you there."

He was working for a small graphic design studio, and I was fresh out of college and hoping to work in campus ministry. WAY back then, the ministry I wanted to work with required that both the husband and wife work together in that ministry. My husband is a very talented designer, artist, creator, filmmaker, and business owner. He was not eager to do what I was passionate about; he had his own, very different passions. He responded, "Let's get as creative as we can. And if we cannot find a solution—I will join you in ministry."

This was the beginning of our lifelong dance of two callings under one roof.

Two different kinds of gifts, job skills, leadership, dreams, hopes all in one marriage. The "two becoming one" of marriage didn't mean we abandoned our whole selves at the altar, forsaking who we were made to be, melting into one other unidentifiable kind of person. Becoming "one" has much more to do with serving one another, putting one another above the other, loving one another, laying down our lives for one another. It means we forsake all others and are united to each other under one King.

And in every season of our marriage there has been a different rhythm to the dance of two callings under one roof.

The Young Married Years:

We got creative and I was able to work on campus, and he worked as a designer. We worked different shifts and figured out ways to be together and build our marriage. It was just us. Flexibility and bending for one another didn't cost us much. We had five years of just us and enjoyed our independence as well as our oneness.

The Baby and Little Years:

So often death must happen to give birth to new life. And the cost of laying down my life came head on with our first child. I was nursing and I was home. It was hard and beautiful and the growing pains of our new adjustment were raw and real. This season (and for all three of our babies) was a time where we both chose to do less. We had more of our own family and less of our own time. With each person added to our family, the cost got higher. My calling grew fuller: Motherhood and Campus Ministry. In this new rhythm we had to figure out how motherhood and my calling fit together. My husband had to do the same. How did being a father and being a creative entrepreneur work together?

At each opportunity we had to ask, "What can I lay down and what can I pick up?" We had to ask God and we had to ask each other. We weren't solo anymore. We were two people under the same roof, and we were one. We had three beautiful souls to care for. And when your marriage is built on Jesus, serving one another in love is a big deal.

By faith, we then chose what to lay down and what to pick up. Sometimes it was beautiful, sometimes it was a hot mess. But we kept asking God, and each other, about using our gifts. Even if it was once a month. Or every day. We kept talking about it and making space for the other's calling/work/dreams.

"I am flying out for work, how can I make this as easy for you as I can?"

"Can I speak at this retreat and you stay with the kids?"

"Thursday evenings are your night. I'll be home with the kids and you can be on campus. Sound good?"

Let's be real—there were many tears, heated discussions, and blame assigned in this phase about whose job trumped whose. Which was the wrong way to see it. We aren't against each other. We are teammates. Working together with two callings under one roof. Regretfully, sometimes we stole from one another to make space for our calling. Turns out gift-giving and creating space for the other to soar works much better. Gift-giving brings life to a marriage.

The School Years:

My day is freeing up a bit more each year, as two of my three kids are in school. Each year at open house, I look every teacher in the eye and say, "Thank you. Thank you for being passionate about your calling." I watch these teachers love my kids, teach them amazing things about algebra and the Bill of Rights, and expand their world in all kinds of ways. It's a beautiful village. There are women teaching in our school system that I mentored and coached in college, and it's this lovely cycle of giving and growing. Everyone using their gifts in our village.

Currently:

I continue to watch my motherhood and ministry

weave together. My full calling pushes and pulls and expands and gives grace to itself. My firstborn son now wants me to practice my ministry talks, sermons, and seminars on him; he wants to listen in. He claps when I'm done and cheers me on. What fun to see my children want me to do a good job with my gifts! My children are watching their mom make space for their dad, and their dad carve out space for their mom. They are watching gift-giving and two callings in one marriage. That's one of the best gifts I can give them.

So dearest married couple: you can hold all kinds of dreams and callings and hopes together. Some need to lay low for a season. Some must die altogether to give birth to new ones. Some need to be refined. It might take a village of callings to make them all work. But listen and ask questions and make space and room for each other. Find out what the dreams are. Have they changed? What season are you in? What dreams are underneath your husband's hard work? Lay things down. Give your spouse and yourself the gifts of time, space, listening ears and an open heart. See what life comes when we give gifts freely to one another. May you, by faith, move mountains for two callings under one roof.

~

In our lifelong dance of two callings under one roof we have a lot to think through. We need good, thoughtful questions to ask one another. We need to look at how opportunity and gifts intersect. We need to think through our motherhood and our fatherhood and who our children are and find the sweet spot for every season. Which seems like some weird algorithm, but God knows. And remember, He leads, carries, feeds and holds us in this.

As we live this out, let's be very aware of the subtle lies crouching in corners, looking to steal the joy of our dance. Here are three lies (among many) that come with the territory:

The Lie: He is out there living his dreams and is always doing amazing things at work. I am stuck here at home wiping butts or doing a job that does not further any of my dreams.

The Truth: Each and every job has toil. No one is always doing amazing things and firing on all cylinders all the time. "Always" will be the death of us, sister. Our world is fallen and there is toil during our days. The ground is cursed and things are hard.

Every one of us wrestles like King Solomon: "I have seen all the things that are done under the sun; all of them are meaningless, a chasing after the wind." Each job has its beauty and its mire. The mire doesn't make it less meaningful, but it's not glamorous either.

Just like I had the joy of being the one to watch all three of my children's first steps while my husband was at work, he had the joy of creating an award-winning piece in his industry. And just like I can drown in the household organization and management of schedules and tantrums, he is worn out in the travel, in the long meetings, and the negative work attitudes. Just as I feel like I am doing what I am made to do when I write and speak, so my husband feels that same thing as he creates and makes all kinds of things. But I don't teach often. And my husband doesn't soar every work day.

The Lie: Wiping butts, building Legos, doing puzzles, reading books, and fill in the blank of your own madness in motherhood is small and insignificant.

The Truth: As we parent (for very long hours and with repetition and toil) we are in the image of God. This is no small thing. We may not be soaring in our strengths as we fold laundry, but we must remember, dear friend, we are doing a God-activity called Maintaining and Sustaining. We must not become tripped up by this lie, fall into the trap that only certain things are significant, and cry ourselves to sleep nightly. Each day is teeming with opportunity to walk around passing out faith, hope, and love like candy. Let's get after it.

Children are quite significant. They are gifts. They are blessings. They are like arrows in the hand of a warrior, remember? They have dignity, value, and worth. They are absolutely worth the mundane. They are worth the madness. They are worth the endless (death machine) laundry and lunch packing and toilet cleaning. Each day we maintain and sustain their lives with faith, hope, love and laughter, we are like God. This is big, good news. And these young arrows? They will be our next presidents, educators, and world changers. Let us fill their affection tanks. Their confidence tanks. Their significance tanks to the brim and overflowing and watch them soar when we launch them into the world!

The Lie: I am the only one sacrificing.

The Truth: When two people become one, everyone compromises. Everyone sacrifices. Many things are laid down. As well, many joys are picked up. Would my husband prefer, in light of his hopes and dreams, to be on the west coast pursuing filmmaking and furthering his dreams? Yes. Many days, yes. But has he sacrificed this and laid down that aspiration for this season because of our family life? Yes. The joy of coming home to three kids who can't wait to wrestle and kiss him is magnificent. Would I prefer, many days, to be teaching, speaking, writing, mentoring, and coaching adults in their spiritual growth? Yes. But have I set much of that aside for a season, as a personal decision? Yes. And the joy of being present to read, snuggle, chase, and laugh is precious. Have

I slowly given more time to my calling as my three children have grown? Yes. Have I wrestled with what is helpful for our family, for my calling, for my man's calling each season of each child in our family? Yes.

And for the record, do I think there is a one-size-fits-all way to working and motherhood? No. Each of our motherhood dresses come in various shapes and sizes, so each one of us looks so very different as we mother best for our family and circumstances. I want to enjoy how motherhood looks on others all around me. I want to come alongside, lift up, and learn from all my friends who stay at home, work from home, work part-time and work full-time for all kinds of reasons. We each have to decide, with our spouse, what this looks like and why. Of course it will change and ebb and flow per season. May freedom and grace abound. There are plenty of both.

Perspective is our wise friend when merging callings under one roof. If you find yourself spiraling downward, ready to shoot the one you love for any number of reasons, then slow down and see what you find. Shift to see the gifts, the joys, the sweetness. Inhale grace. Exhale frustration. Are there lies? What exactly are you believing? Is there joy? What are those joys?

Then fight to find the truth. Assess before you accuse. Put down the "never" and the "always" and the fists and the dagger eyes, and see what is reality.

Shift to see truth.

Shift to see the gifts.

Shift to see the joys.

Chin up, friend. We can make room for two callings and we can do it with faith, hope, and love.

As Pharaoh approached, the Israelites looked up, and there were the Egyptians, marching after them. They were terrified and cried out to the Lord. They said to Moses, "Was it because there were no graves in Egypt that you brought us to the desert to die? What have you done to us by bringing us out of Egypt? Didn't we say to you in Egypt, 'Leave us alone; let us serve the Egyptians'? It would have been better for us to serve the Egyptians than to die in the desert!" Moses answered the people, "Do not be afraid. Stand firm and you will see the deliverance the Lord will bring you today. The Egyptians you see today you will never see again. The Lord will fight for you; you need only to be still.

—Exodus 14:10–14

11

I Will Fight for You

I was finally in my car, alone. Thank God. It had been a poke-your-eye-out-day of carpooling, meal-making, time-outing. I was trying not to watch the clock, fighting to stay present. But sometimes looking forward to a break can boost your sails and keep you afloat. No shame in the anticipation of something refreshing. When the time came to grab my overnight bag, my talk for the women's group, and the address for the two hour away city, I was very ready. I love me some Seiffert kids and the faith, hope, and loving, and I ALSO love me some alone time in the car with some podcasts and prayer. Sans whining, crying, and general angst.

Driving down the highway, with the late afternoon sun behind me, I prayed two thoughts: God, please speak to the women through me. And God, please speak to me through the women. It was weird to ask Him to speak to me in this situation, since I was coming to encourage them. But, oddly, it felt like He nudged me to ask Him. So I did, and kept on driving to the destination.

A dear friend had asked me to come speak to her mom's group months before, in the autumn. Which was right around the time when I was the most tired in motherhood that I could remember; motherhood was maddening and I was fighting to keep my chin up. I had done everything I knew to try to be my healthiest self. I had sat with a counselor (again), was eating clean, was exercising each morning, was reading God's truth daily. All of these combined was not enough. I was certainly not enough, again.

It seems there are seasons in life where extra helpings of grace are needed. Where even the regular, everyday grace feels out of reach, and the days are gray, hard, and void of hope. I had hoped it was the cold winter that had put me in this place, and that soon, spring and sunshine would bring me back. Ohio can break a mom in February. Spring had finally arrived, beauty was budding, warm weather showed up. But I was unable to reach out and enjoy all the new life around me. I struggled. Every day felt like a mountain I had to climb and I had just traversed the same territory the day before. Defeat made residence within my heart.

I mentioned, competition is one of my strengths. However, over the past few years I had come to see this strength as mostly a selfish, annoying characteristic. The description (from StrengthFinders) seemed like it was about me winning against others and rising to the top in as many situations as possible. Competition did not seem spiritual.

As it turns out, competition was one of the most spiritual and useful gifts God had given me. I just had not shifted enough to see it. We won't find "competition" listed alongside apostle, prophet, evangelist. It's not in the Bible as a "spiritual gift"—not like that kind. This gift was the kind that gave me fight in the face of fear, grit in the grip of gray. Competition came in handy as I lay in bed each morning and was face to face with the day. The day challenged me, dared me, taunted me to get up and try to take it on. The day told me it was too much for me, motherhood was too loud and crazy, that the lists and the schedules and the driving and the book bags and the soccer cleats were going to outlast me. The day tried to tell me it had me beat before I put my feet on the floor.

I didn't know it was depression. All I knew was that I didn't want to get out of bed. But I still did. Because I wasn't going down like that, and if I didn't get up, who was going to do that for me? I was the only mom in the house, and my competitive nature took that as a challenge. I fought my defeat, beat back my depressing thoughts, and got out of bed. I kept doing this, over months, and I became bone-tired. Exhausted. Motherhood on me at this point felt like a worn thin, ragged dress. Faded and colorless.

So I started casually wondering out loud to friends. Sometimes I think, I might possibly be, depressed? This seemed hard for those around me to swallow. I was functioning, doing all that was on my plate, laughing around others. Competent extroverts might have the hardest time being believed in as they share about depression. We look like we are doing great! We are the life of the party, we have energy around others, we are still getting stuff done! But when people (adult people) were gone, so was my energy and motivation. Loving my children well and playing with them was like pushing water uphill. Add laundry to my day, and we have death itself.

So my prayer on the drive to speak to this women's group became, "God please speak to them, and please speak to me." More specifically, I was asking God's permission to take antidepressants. God's permission? This may seem like a weird idea to some of you. But if you have been around the Christian culture for any extended period of time, things can get lopsided. They often don't mean to, but ideas can get off-kilter because we are messy humans. Some of you know all too well what I am talking about. Where if you are sick, it's because you don't have enough faith. If something isn't working in your life, then you need to confess some kind of sin. If you take depression meds, you are now relying on the medical field instead of trusting in Jesus. And you're in danger of your soul rotting and all hell breaking loose. But I digress.

I asked God's permission because something seemed broken, unfixable, torn. I had run out of solutions, run out of myself. I wondered if medicine was a good option. And once again, God's ever faithful words stood up, climbed my mountain, and offered a strong hand down to me: "My grace is enough; my power is made perfect in your weakness."

There again. Always with the grace. This time grace poured down like fresh spring rain, washing away months, possibly years, of grime off of fogged up thoughts. All while I was speaking to this sweet group of moms.

I spoke to those women that evening and tears streamed down their cheeks from the truth and grace that washed over them. And then it was my turn. Turning into smaller groups, they asked what I wanted prayer for. It was as if God had set the table and was just waiting for me to accept His invitation to enjoy the goodness. "I am struggling with depression and I want to be free to take antidepressants." Two women prayed with me, one was a student who had been in my ministry and had become a counselor (I'm like a proud little mama when I see former college students thriving). The other was a trusted friend, as safe as your favorite blanket growing up. God had positioned these women to hear me and pray for me at this exact moment in my life. I shifted in my seat and saw the gifts of these girls, this place, this evening in front of me.

They prayed for me and my friend said, "As I was praying for you, I feel like God is saying this: 'You are a fighter. But let me fight for you.'"

Nothing sweeter could have ever been whispered to my withered soul. Nothing more perfect and direct. Nothing more healing than the meds themselves. I was a fighter. He made me that way. But it was time to let Him fight for me. He knew who I was. He knew my name. He handcrafted me and gave me skills. And I could rest. He had come to my rescue.

Later that evening, after the chatter and the cake and the catching up, I hunted down the words from a Psalm I had forgotten. The Psalms are balms to our human, ragged soul. They are poems where we overhear humans talk to God, we listen in as they coach

their souls into knowing what is true. Read this one
carefully, friend, and let it sink down deep.

> I love you, O Lord, my strength.
> The Lord is my rock and my fortress and my deliverer,
> my God, my rock, in whom I take refuge,
> my shield, and the horn of my salvation,
> my stronghold.
> I call upon the Lord, who is worthy to be praised,
> and I am saved from my enemies.
> The cords of death encompassed me;
> the torrents of destruction assailed me the cords of
> Sheol entangled me;
> the snares of death confronted me.
> In my distress I called upon the Lord;
> to my God I cried for help.
> From his temple he heard my voice,
> and my cry to him reached his ears.
> Then the earth reeled and rocked;
> the foundations also of the mountains trembled
> and quaked, because he was angry.
> Smoke went up from his nostrils,
> and devouring fire from his mouth;
> glowing coals flamed forth from him.
> He bowed the heavens and came down;
> thick darkness was under his feet.
> He rode on a cherub and flew;

he came swiftly on the wings of the wind.

He made darkness his covering,
his canopy around him,
thick clouds dark with water.
Out of the brightness before him
hailstones and coals of fire broke through his clouds.
The Lord also thundered in the heavens,
and the Most High uttered his voice,
hailstones and coals of fire.
And he sent out his arrows and scattered them;
he flashed forth lightnings and routed them.
Then the channels of the sea were seen,
and the foundations of the world were laid bare
at your rebuke, O Lord,
at the blast of the breath of your nostrils.
He sent from on high, he took me;
he drew me out of many waters.
He rescued me from my strong enemy
and from those who hated me,
for they were too mighty for me.
They confronted me in the day of my calamity,
but the Lord was my support.
He brought me out into a broad place;
he rescued me, because he delighted in me.
—Psalm 18:1–19

David, the writer of Psalm 18, nailed it. Can we

give God any more possible names for strength and security? No, we cannot. These will most certainly do: Rock, Fortress, Rescuer, Deliverer, Shield, Refuge, Stronghold. We watch David cry out against his enemies and God responds with might. He hears David, sees David, and He moves for David. God sends out arrows, lightning, fire, hail—He is pulling out all the stops. And then He pulls out David himself from the many waters and rescued him. Rescue is the theme, and the reason is because God delights in him. In you. In me.

I owned this Psalm, and I practiced telling my soul, "He rescues me, because He delights in me. He fought for David, He will fight for me." I embraced the truth that God hears me, sees me, and He moves for me.

Antidepressants have proven to be absolutely beautiful. I never thought I would find grace from a pill, but I have. Defeating the looming feeling of getting out of bed is real. The mounding anxiety has gone quiet. And this is my favorite—my husband has said a few times that I just "feel lighter to him." Thank the good Lord. How heavy did I feel before? Did I have postpartum depression that just went unchecked...through three babies? It seems something got out of sorts, and I couldn't sort it out. But Jesus, community, antidepressants, exercise, good food... these are good gifts.

What have you been fighting? What has worn you down? Do you know He delights in you and wants to rescue you? Friend, I want you to know you can rest now. You can put down your sword, turn in your shield, take off your helmet. God is the One who does not sleep, defeats our enemies, and delights in you. Be free, sister. Grace covers us when we expose all of our ugliness, limitations, issues. We can walk with our head held high and a cape of grace trailing behind us.

Chin up, God will fight for you. God will defeat your enemies. God delights in you.

*"Though our feelings come and go,
God's love for us does not."*

—C.S. Lewis

12

The Good Part

Classic. She's huffing and puffing in the kitchen and zipping around like a ping pong ball. Overcommitted, overwhelmed, and over it, this mom is starting to lose it with the party prep. How is it party days can bring out our demons? Thirty people will be arriving in a few hours and NO ONE IS HELPING.

What sounded like fun a few days ago turned into a personal bitter-fest. She is growing bitter at all the chopping of vegetables, all the wiping down of who knows what from the countertops, all the party things. Sure, her husband asks what he can do to help. But she hisses out "Nothing!" and swiftly shuts him down. Translation: "Why can't you just look around and start doing things? Why can't you see the living room needs picked up and vacuumed, the floor has smashed grapes and Cheez-Its from yesterday ground into it, and my 'Party Day!' List is hanging on the center of the fridge so everyone can see all the woes. Do you really care? Time is ticking. Just PICK a job!"

Maybe she's me. OK, fine, she's me. But I'm going to bank on her being you, too. We volunteer to host a big thing a few months out, and it feels really charming and quite easy in our mind. However, three days before the actual event, we start sweating. We question everything from our house to our hair. Why did I do this? I can't possibly make it the perfectly perfect thing that is in my mind! Can I fake an injury? Should I just throw myself out a window, break a leg, and rely on the pity of a friend? WHY, God? WHY?

This dumpster fire of inner turmoil is actually a scene in the Bible. Before you guess the key players, take a breath. Vow to see it through fresh eyes if you've seen it a thousand times. If you've never read this brief story, then this one is for you, sister.

Now as they went on their way, Jesus entered a village. And a woman named Martha welcomed him into her house. And she had a sister called Mary, who sat at the Lord's feet and listened to his teaching. But Martha was distracted with much serving. And she went up to him and said, "Lord,

*do you not care that my sister has left me to serve
alone? Tell her then to help me." But the Lord
answered her, "Martha, Martha, you are anxious
and troubled about many things, but one thing
is necessary. Mary has chosen the good portion,
which will not be taken away from her."*
—Luke 10:38–42

Martha starts out bubbling over with great intentions and warmth: "She welcomed Jesus into her house." She's killing it at this point. Flinging open the doors of her home and her heart, she invited Jesus right on in. Yep, I feel ya sister. I have had fantastic motives when I first sign up to take something on in my home. I am warm, welcoming, willing.

But then, Mary. She is literally JUST SITTING THERE. Get serious. What in the world is wrong with her? Can't she see all the things that have to happen? And this is back in Bible times where they had electric nothing and Pinterest decor was not the problem. They were kneading their own bread, roasting lambs, pressing olives, cutting up pomegranates. Bible food prep is no joke. A quick run to Aldi was right out.

Enter bitterness. What the what, Jesus? Don't you care? If she were texting Jesus from the back of the kitchen to avoid actual conversation, an eye-roll emoji or the red mad-face guy would definitely be in there.

"Tell her to help me, Jesus. I am alone. I am helpless. I am mad. Eye-roll guy."

How many times do we feel this way in our own kitchens, cars, living rooms, or showers (during a good shower-cry, of course)? Overcommitted. Unsupported. Bitter. Blaming others. Blaming God. We question if anyone, Jesus included, actually sees the situation, notices the crazy, understands the fears in our motherhood and in our lives. I am so often Martha. Classic, raw, frustrated Martha.

Jesus replies with tender truth. He sees her, and shepherds her: "Martha, Martha, you are anxious and troubled about many things, but one thing is necessary. Mary has chosen the good portion, which will not be taken away from her."

I love the way the NASB translation says it: "Martha, Martha, you are worried and bothered about so many things; but only one thing is necessary, for Mary has chosen the good part, which shall not be taken away from her."

You are worried and bothered about so many things.

Shoot.

Worried: What will people think of me if I cannot pull this off, if I cannot live up to the standard I have set for myself? What if I am not perfect in this?

Bothered: Anxiety and fear are the major players

here. I am plagued by anxious thoughts and riddled with fears.

So Many Things: If I am not in control of my mind and my emotions, then the to-do list piles as high as my anxiety. My appearance, my performance, and my shame will taunt me.

Jesus cuts straight to Martha's heart condition with her worried and bothered self: "...only one thing is necessary, for Mary has chosen the good part, which shall not be taken away from her."

I had always wondered at "The Good Part" that Mary has chosen. I didn't get it. How was this supposed to work in my everyday motherhood? Is The Good Part just sitting and reading my Bible and accomplishing nothing all day long—our equivalent to Mary listening to Jesus at His feet? This seems utterly unrealistic as a mom. As a woman. As any human person. Surely this is not what Jesus is suggesting we all do, all the time. Children would be starving, neglected, and things would be really, really bad. But that's what The Good Part looked like to me in this passage.

But then, let's come back to my Everyday Spirituality class, the one that refocused my life: "What was so right about Mary's inaction? Very little. What was Jesus' concern? It is more important to let God minister to us than to minister for God."—Paul Stevens

Letting God minister to me is more important than me ministering for God? I had to breathe this out.

Exhale: I minister FOR God.

Inhale: Let God minister TO me.

This concept was gold. And completely counterintuitive. Over the last decade, I had grown accustomed to doing things FOR others. Working in ministry was doing things for God. Becoming a mom was doing things for my babies. Contributing to my community as preschool president and a wide variety of other volunteer things was doing things for others. Everything was for someone, for something.

Let God minister to me, without me doing one darn thing? Can we do that? Yes, we can. At any point in our day, we can. We can choose The Good Part right in the middle of our kitchen madness, our shuttling to soccer practice, our huffing and puffing in our heart.

Choosing The Good Part can look like recognizing our annoyance, our anxiety, our lack of support and asking what's this FOR? Is it for my image, for my fame, or for my hope that God will accept me today? We must find the FOR. Maybe even confess the FOR. And then stop, breathe, and ask God to speak TO you. Minister TO you. Be a friend TO you. This subtle difference can shift our very life. Because God will show up. He longs to speak to the ones He made and loves.

Being ministered to is a heart posture we can always access. Of course we can't just sit there all day; but we can bend our heart, keep our chin up, and let His face shine upon us at any moment. We can let Him love us, let His truth sink down deep, let one verse wash over and over and over us as He ministers to us right there. We can stop the FOR THEM and let the TO ME begin.

Just to be clear, sitting at the feet of Jesus is quite valuable. If we take the time to sit before God and read His truth in the quiet, we will easily recall truth in the middle of crazy. When we are bustling around and on the edge of bitter, we can ask God to speak to us through His beautiful truths. So much truth is collected in the quiet.

Recently I felt left out and vulnerable in a social situation. My natural response was to buzz around my house, pretending to organize, but actually just replaying the scene in my mind. Seeking comfort and stability, I was about to zip off a text to a friend and, unbelievably, I didn't send it. Stopping, I stood completely still, with my children still buzzing around me, and chose to ask God about it. I got quiet in the crazy. The verse I had been chewing on for days came right to my mind:

I love you, God—you make me strong.

God is bedrock under my feet,
the castle in which I live,
my rescuing knight.
My God—the high crag
where I run for dear life,
hiding behind the boulders,
safe in the granite hideout.
—Psalm 18

The Good Part was right there, in the middle of my muddy mind—in the middle of my motherhood madness. God is the very castle in which I live, my rescuing Knight. His peace and truth calmed my anxiety. I needed to know I was safe from what other people thought of me, tucked away in a granite hideout of a mighty God. I craved a King who delivered me from my fears, and I clung to my rescuing Knight. I let God minister to me. I breathed. I did nothing to earn this relational moment with God. Letting anxiety fall to the ground like an old familiar shirt, I held my chin up and basked in the truth that I was safe from other's opinions and judgments. I stood there, dressed in grace, wrapped in love, held together by hope, quiet before the King. The castle imagery was exactly what I was thirsty for in my soul; had I not asked, I am not sure what kind of stunt I would have pulled to make myself feel safe and secure.

Stevens is spot on. Jesus' concern is not that we are inactive and unproductive. His concern is that we let God minister to us. This is far more important, far sweeter, far better, and far more healing. Then, when we do reach out toward others and help, when we do things for God and for others, His shepherding care will simply flow over from us onto them.

Chin up, Momma. The Good Part is letting God love us, speak to us, enjoy us without doing a darn thing for Him.

"Being a mother is learning about strengths you didn't know you had and dealing with fears you didn't know existed."

—Linda Wooten

13

Dear Mom at Target

Dear Mom at Target,

I see you, friend.

I recognize the "just make it through this hour" face. I get why you might have thought the $2 buttery popcorn for your kids was a great option so you can shop, but now you are regretting it because every worker can follow your trail like Hansel and Gretel. It's the worst. I know the exhaustion of so much actual parenting, when all you want to do is look at the new patterns on the throw pillows. Is this too much to ask? No, it is not. Well, it might be...with your three littles in tow. Solidarity. I spot the worn-out motherhood dress. I know how you are considering your escape.

Have you ever considered that God chose a woman to bring about the greatest rescue plan in the world? Not just any woman, a young mom. Like yourself. He chose a mom to birth His son, who would then take on our crap and save us from our sin and separation. He came to bridge the gap between us and God. But He used a young mom to get this whole party started. A beautiful, broken vessel for His light to come through. Quite literally. I know you're in Target, but right now you need soul courage, since your kid just opened a box of tampons and is using them as drumsticks.

Which is fine. No one cares.

Can I offer a roadmap that I began to cling to awhile ago, starting with a 50,000 foot view? It's the big picture. Stay in it with me—it's good. I promise.

When Eve, the first mother, chose to eat that fruit and give some to her husband, she chose to be her own queen (something we know NOTHING about). She chose to disobey the one command from the one true Creator and King. From then on out we ALL have been born into a great rebellion against God as King.

We are born wanting to be our own kings and queens. And this rebellion separates us from God. Although WE are at fault, rejecting God as King and sinning against Him, GOD chose to do something about that mess.

Take heart, friend. He chose a mother. Just like you.

The gender that started the domino effect of sin and rebellion would be the gender for the domino effect of grace and redemption. The domino effect of His unmerited favor. Of His undeserved kindness. Of His gift we don't pay for. And this metanarrative is just one big gift after another: God's grace upon grace. By God's grace, He chose a mother to bring salvation.

After Eve eats the forbidden fruit, then come curses for everyone—The Snake, Eve and Adam. God, right away, starts with the snake's curse:

Because you've done this, you're cursed,
cursed beyond all cattle and wild animals,
Cursed to slink on your belly
and eat dirt all your life.
I'm declaring war between you and the Woman,
between your offspring and hers.
He'll crush your head,
you'll wound his heel.
—Genesis 3

This is getting deep, sister. Your kid is climbing up one of the endcaps, but it's the clearance stuff with the red price stickers, and that's the best. There's grace. Let's not set the bar too high, he's definitely still breathing. Big picture.

"He'll crush your head, you'll wound his heel." The "He" here is the offspring of the woman. Right here we have the first Messianic prophecy—the foretelling of Jesus. War is declared between the Woman and Satan, and she will be his demise. God could have chosen any path He wanted to save people from their sin and He, remarkably, chose motherhood.

Childbearing becomes a centerpiece of the story. Which seems just about right in our own motherhood—it's where it all begins. Eve's curse is that she will have pain in childbearing. But childbearing will also be where redemption starts. Such a beautiful poetry in it all. Pain with a purpose. God chose a broken human vessel—a mother—and put His Son inside of her.

She was stretched out by Salvation.

She grew Grace in her womb.

She gave birth to Redemption.

We watch all this through Mary, who gets the gift of redeeming the curse of Eve. This is recorded in Matthew 1:20–21:

> *God's angel spoke to Joseph in the dream, "Joseph, son of David, don't hesitate to get married. Mary's pregnancy is Spirit-conceived. God's Holy Spirit has made her pregnant. She will bring a son to*

birth, and when she does, you, Joseph, will name him Jesus—'God saves'—because he will save his people from their sins."

He chose a young mom to do something phenomenal and world changing.

He chose a young mom to bring beauty and hope and redemption and grace.

He chose a young mom to shower with gifts and kindness.

Yes, your children have now ruined many Target pillows with their butterfingers. But you, sister, swim in the same stream as Eve and Mary. This is big. Perfect Eden and Curses and Holy Mary and the Birth of the Savior and You.

If I could, I would meet you on the Target roof with a helicopter and whisk you way up high to see how small your red cart and your kids' tantrums and your worries are, compared to the grand view God has given us from the creation of the world until now. Those things are real, but they are small when we lift up our eyes to the King and view His grand plan.

Oh, and one more thing, sweet momma. What I love is that God continually longs to be gracious to us. It wasn't a one-time-only gift of grace. His grace is present and active. We see countless times that God's character is one of continual grace-giving. It started by not punishing us for our sin and even transferring our punishment upon His son. Jesus wrote the check and paid for it. And His grace keeps on coming. We are finding it everywhere.

Let's take our tattered, butter-stained motherhood dresses to the King, with all the holes and flaws, and let Him mend them with grace. Won't it be fun to show off how grace covers over the ways motherhood didn't fit before? To boast in our weaknesses, so God's power is perfected? Yes, it will be. I have really started to enjoy showing off God's grace in my motherhood.

Chin up, the big picture is so good for our souls.

With all my love and respect,
A mom one step further down the road

*"Every child deserves a champion:
an adult who will never give up on
them, who understands the power of
connection and insists they become
the best they can possibly be."*

—Rita Pierson

*"No matter what people tell you, words
and ideas can change the world."*

—Robin Williams

14

Orphans

She was playing with dolls, combing cornsilk hair, fluffing their dresses. The gentle hum of her voice singing softly. Her song was simple and sweet, but the words were too quiet for me to catch. I rounded the corner right when her voice gained an unexpected strength as she clearly sang four bold words, "You make me brave."

I completely lost it. I turned around, opened the refrigerator, and cried into the cool shelves. Tears dripped down onto tomatoes. The milk and I had a moment.

This sweet little foster girl has witnessed things she should never have seen. She's heard things her ears shouldn't hold. She absolutely has every right to sing a prayer-song asking to be brave. She's here in my living room, safe, and yes, brave. God has already made her brave and will continue to do so.

As I heard her sing, I wiped my tears, and got to work. We must have truth and love displayed all over this safe place, I told myself. I got out my Bible and went straight to the worn page that read:

She is clothed with strength and dignity and laughs at the future.
—Proverbs 31:25

Walking over to my art room, I found my favorite marker. I cradled my Bible and found the butcher paper roll that is fixed to our kitchen wall, and wrote each word from this verse carefully, gently.

All I hoped for this little girl in my care was wrapped up in this verse. I wanted to clothe her in the best attire we could afford. The kind of dress that doesn't wear out, always looks beautiful, and never fails. The kind of dress stitched with love, strength, dignity, laughter, and grace.

Did she grapple with how her childhood-dress was fitting? Were we similar, as I continued to make amends with my motherhood-dress, owning God's grace that covers what I'd rather hide? Will we both look at this verse on my kitchen wall and let God stitch His truths over us?

Will we rehearse the same speech in the mirror?

"Today I put on STRENGTH AND DIGNITY, y'all. Stand back. Cuz I'm coming through wearing the King's clothes. You bet my chin is up. That's the only way to wear dignity, and strength only fits when our head is held high." I hoped and prayed we would wear our new clothes in our minds and hearts.

Several years ago, as I watched friends around me become licensed foster care parents, it felt like its own special beast. You had to have guts and kindness and boundaries and love all at the same time for SEVERAL hours strung together. You had to love others, on top of loving your own biological children and their wily ways. Who can do this?!

Not me!

This looked like crazy town. The families I knew in my city who were fostering were dear to me, and I admired them. I watched them stretch bedrooms to make space and extend tables to serve the broken. They had extra schedules to manage, speech therapy to arrange, advocating to do, and so many mouths to feed (since sibling groups are kept together as best as possible in foster care). It all seemed like a beautiful mess. But not a mess I was willing to enter.

Then God brought it up to me. Like the kind of bringing up where you just keep thinking about the orphan, and then you run into what God thinks about taking care of the abused, the neglected, and the downtrodden in His word. And then you add in my personality that has this weird mix of part shepherd and part CEO—and you consider it.

I know what you're thinking. She has been writing about how motherhood has been her weakest place, her crooked dress, and she is offering to take in more? To take in broken, messy, neglected or abused children? To bring in a child with a background that has many question marks?

Yep.

However. This is where the trust fall comes in, every time. If God is nudging my soul about anything, I would rather try and trust Him than miss the gift. Even if the gift is just the actual trusting of God. His way is worth it to me. His way is higher. His way is above my small thinking.

My husband had been willing to foster children for a long time. I often think Rob should apply to be a SAHD. He'd get the job. He'd be amazing at it. His heart is naturally calm, and his mind is steady. But if he stayed at home, we most likely would have to move in with my parents. So that's out.

When I brought up taking foster care classes, he was all in. Just like that. But I still needed convincing, even though I felt a God-nudge, and I was the one looking into all the details to get our license. Then one afternoon this verse jumped off the page at me:

*God is able to make all grace abound to you, so
that having all sufficiency in all things at all times,
you may abound in every good work.*
—*2 Corinthians 9:8*

I couldn't get over the "all's."

All grace.

All sufficiency.

All things.

All times.

He was making it clear to me that His ALL covered my step of faith to foster others. It covered all my fear. All my hesitations. All my excuses. All means all.

The Message reads this same verse this way, "God can pour on the blessings in astonishing ways so that you're ready for anything and everything, more than just ready to do what needs to be done."

This was a beautiful, grace-filled message for my journey in housing the underprivileged and neglected. So we went for it, took the 36 hours of classes, and opened our hearts and home. We now do a lot of Respite Care, which is taking children who are currently in foster homes for up to two weeks. Often this is so the foster family can go on vacation, get a break, or actually be investigated because things aren't adding up.

With each child or sibling pair we have in our

home, I wrap myself in strength and dignity and bank on all the grace and all the sufficiency for all the days we have them in our home. Because fostering isn't something I had dreamed about for years; each hour is faith-filled. I start sweating each time I see our agency calling; I perspire for the first 24–48 hours as I try to trust Jesus with new faces and hard stories. I am surprised to say each situation has gone way better than anticipated, and we have been thankful for every child.

Watching my children share their rooms, their favorite toys, and their hearts has been one of my favorite parts. They have bent to bless, have been flexible by faith. And this has not been without injury. My son has been stolen from, and we questioned his honesty in the middle of the mess. My daughter has cried watching her toys get mistreated, her world get upended. My youngest had to find his voice and shout that he doesn't want anyone to pick him up anymore.

My heart has been broken into a million pieces when I've heard some children tell their stories. Some have casually shared being chased into the woods with garden tools. Others have told about the gut-wrenching day they were removed from their homes with police and shouting and confusion. Caring for the orphan is completely overwhelming if we don't stay grounded in grace. If we don't wear strength. If we don't don dignity.

But this verse Paul writes isn't to guilt you into becoming a foster parent. That's not how I roll, nor how God does. God's grace and abundance covers any step of faith we make, making us more than ready to do whatever it is in front of us. To do whatever is placed on our hearts in our motherhood. To dream, to try things, and to trust God.

We are mothers, and we mother in so many ways. We mother our own children and the neighborhood ones that multiply like rabbits in our backyard. We mother babies and littles and middles and lost teens. We mother college students with a meal and a listening ear, maybe even a room for a while. We mother both people and ideas. We mother orphans and orphaned dreams, left-behind concepts, hidden-away hopes. When we mother both people and ideas, we watch the world change.

Is there some passion inside of you that needs nurtured and loved, cared for and watered? Is God asking you to use the gifts He has put inside of you to develop the ideas in your heart? Is He nudging you to take a step of outlandish faith, promising you He has ALL grace and ALL sufficiency for you in ALL things and at ALL times?

Throughout my motherhood there have been many moments when I wanted to do something, try out an idea, or cultivate a new skill. But I was afraid to fail and show my weakness. So I kept my ideas close to my chest, closed off and hidden. This is not God's way. He has given us gifts to use and grace to fail. Grace doesn't mean we do something perfectly. Grace means when we fail, we are loved, and we can get our chin up and try again. Grace is abounding, sufficient, enough.

How many amazing and life changing ideas would our world have missed, had not someone cared for and nurtured these concepts? Had not someone taken that dream, hope, or skill, and watered it, pouring life into it? We would have missed so much philosophy, anthropology, and psychology. We would be lacking stories that anchor our souls and ideas that encourage us to fly. We would have missed groundbreaking medicine and soul-arresting beauty. Had we left dreams to die and orphaned our hopes, we would be a small and impoverished world.

There are all kinds of orphans and all kinds of grace. Let us not forget that when we are nudged to care for any kind of orphaned child or any kind of orphaned dream, God has it ALL covered. All the grace to cover all the fear. All the love to cover all the sin. All the strength to cover all the weakness. He will hand us bravery at the same time He awakens dreams. We can boast in our failings as we go and show off the grace-covering we get to wear in our motherhood.

Grace makes all kinds of mothering such a natural fit.

Chin up, friend. God has loved our orphaned hearts and abandoned dreams. He will supply us with love to do the same for ourselves and others.

"If we do not regularly quit work for one day a week we take ourselves far too seriously."

—Eugene Peterson

15

I'm Bringing Sabbath Back

I remember, so often, flopping down on the couch on a Sunday night despairing that Monday was already on the heels of my weekend. Monday was always showing up at the wrong time. The weekends were for cleaning, organizing, gardening, grocery shopping, soccer gaming, errand running, and everything else-ing from Saturday seamlessly into Sunday evening. Both days were to catch-up and buckle-down. As a result I was bluesy, tired, and resistant to a new week. I went to bed unprepared to address another Monday morning.

The Monday Morning Blues are real, and so are The Sunday Night Dreads. We use up our weekend time to organize our possessions, run our children around, and work hard on house projects. We empty our physical and emotional tanks, with Monday's gauge starting on E, and no gas station in sight.

Well into my motherhood I started to hear some chatter about the Sabbath. I wasn't quite sure what it meant, but it sounded lovely. The idea of taking a whole day off each week sounded ideal, and definitely impossible. It's not like I could quit being a mom for one day a week. Well, I could, but that's called neglect.

I couldn't afford to stop anyway. My world was spinning, and if I let go, if I relaxed, it would fall off its axis, spin out of orbit and we would all be doomed. We would most certainly all die. If I was honest, I believed I kept the world spinning.

Eugene Peterson challenged my thinking, "Sabbath is uncluttered time and space to distance ourselves from the frenzy of our own activities so we can see what God has been and is doing. If we do not regularly quit work for one day a week we take ourselves far too seriously. The moral sweat pouring off our brows blinds us to the primal action of God in and around us. We have a culture that ignores time, it's just another commodity to be consumed. Because we live in a world that is ignorant of the work of God, we over-estimate the work of man."—Eugene Peterson

Some of Peterson's words ping-ponged around my brain, hitting established thoughts and confronting patterns in my world:

Uncluttered time and space. That was a cool glass of water to my parched situation. Was it possible? Could we have uncluttered anything?

Distance ourselves from the frenzy. I am the frenzy, so it may prove to be challenging to take a break from me. But, I want distance from frenzy either way.

We take ourselves far too seriously. Touché. Could I actually trust God to rest an entire day a week? This feels scary to a productive, self-reliant person.

Time is just another commodity to consume. Guilty. I usually want everything to have a purpose. Hence, life on the floor is a challenge.

Ignorant to God's work, we overestimate man's. Stopping one day a week to reflect on what God has done and is doing, and to lift my chin up to see God— this sounded like medicine to my week.

I started to read about people who had a rhythm of rest and work. Their practices were inspiring, their hearts were clearer, their homes were lighter. Why did they Sabbath, and what allowed them to rest?

What was compelling was that we don't have to look much further than the very first week of Creation. God did some serious making, and some fantastic creating, for six days straight. We watch Him create stars, sky, waters, deserts, mountains, insects, animals, man and woman. He then created rest. He made a day to rest, a rhythm of work and sabbath. I doubt He was tired, from what I know about Him.

He was setting up an order, a way of being, a pattern for His crown of creation to follow. Work hard. Rest well. Repeat. We see God make it one of the Ten Commandments, and later Jesus expounds on it beautifully. He says at the end of the day the Sabbath was made for man, not man for the Sabbath. We get the gift of resting, not a yoke of rules about how we rest or don't rest.

John Piper puts it this way, "Jesus didn't come to abolish the Sabbath but to dig it out from under the mountain of legalistic sediment, and give it to us again as a blessing rather than a burden."

So we set out to Sabbath. We still used our Saturday to do chores, house projects, kids sports and errands. But we also, on Saturday, prepared to rest. We cracked eggs, browned sausage, and put together simple casseroles for Sunday brunch. This was enough for our family plus extras we could invite. Looking ahead to Monday, we got our things ready for the week. As Saturday started to come to a close, we put away all signs of "work." Sometimes it was computers, and sometimes it was yard tools. And so the Sabbath experiment was on.

We set aside 24 hours from Saturday evening to Sunday evening to rest from work. We wanted to value people, our kids, friends, nature, wonder and awe. We wanted to connect with God. Having friends over for fires, getting a good night's sleep, leaving dishes to be done until the end of Sunday—these were a few practices. And naps. All the Sunday naps. When the littles napped, so did we.

It was after one such Sunday nap in winter when I opened my eyes to falling snow, heard only afternoon quiet. Kids were sure to be coming down soon, but for now, it was placid. As it was still silent, I messaged my friend and director of the college ministry I was working with, asking when I was speaking this semester. I was just thinking through the upcoming months.

Still feeling sleepy and slow she replied, "You speak this Thursday. You kick off our first series this semester!"

Like a drunk friend who sobers up instantly when police arrive, I sat straight up. I started sweating. It was Sunday. I spoke at Cru in 4 days. I had NO talk prepared. Zero. Nothing. AND my husband was leaving for the entire week on Monday. Single motherhood and a speaking gig was not the plan.

I fumbled for my computer. Time was not budgeted in my week for this. The time was now. I needed to start writing something for these amazing college students. (Let's be clear, it was absolutely my fault this was not in my calendar, but here I was. Sweating.)

In the middle of my panic, God whispered to my soul, "Didn't you tell Me this morning you would trust Me to take a whole day off? Do you trust Me to take care of you, to provide for you, even in this?"

Friends, this is the whole thing. If we take an entire day to simply stop what we normally do, we do so by faith. To practice the Sabbath is to practice trusting God and to lean entirely on His gift of grace. We trust that He will give us what we need. I had prepared for the Sabbath. I got the things done needed to be ready to rest, but THIS was a face-off with the King.

I had a choice: do I scramble or do I Sabbath?

It took all of my strength, grit, and grace to close my computer and push it across the just-napped-on couch. As I pushed away my work, I pulled in Jesus. I slowly told Him I would Sabbath and trust Him to come through for me and write my talk this week.

Friends, I kid you not, the moment I prayed that surrender prayer, He reminded me of a blog post I wrote earlier that fall. The title of my post was the very same title of my assigned Cru talk for the week. It was the weirdest. Like, Jesus-awesome-weird.

Tears dripped onto the warm pillow, down into the crevice of the couch, falling where my body had rested.

My tears from trusting Him were like the manna bread the Israelites used to receive on the seventh day, His provision raining down from the sky. Each morning while wandering in the desert, the Israelites gathered manna (weird wafer-like bread) that God provided for them. On the sixth day, they gathered an extra day's work. This bread literally fell from the sky, straight from Heaven. God provided exactly what they needed. They didn't have to work to get their food on the Sabbath.

I rested, and He gave me extra. He showed up with a basketful of grace, per usual.

For the Israelites, the idea of a Sabbath could have been just as frightening to them as it is for us, maybe more. This is definitely daunting in our efficient and productivity driven culture. In our lives that can't handle not doing anything. In our overscheduled calendars. But for the Israelites, can you imagine the other cultures around them, working hard and farming and gathering food—the most basic and necessary thing (because, no Aldi)—and the Israelite God has told them to rest from this work one day each week?

Something they had to ask themselves was: If He is truly God, is He big enough to be God when we do nothing to provide food, nourishment, and sustenance for ourselves?

That question is real. And hard. And if we practice

a day of rest, we have to ask it, too. We might have to ask it multiple times that day, keeping us connected to God, our chin up, and our minds fixed on what He is doing.

What a beautiful thing it has been to cease the belief that I make things happen in my world, and to remember that God is our provider, maintainer, and sustainer. What a gift it has been to remember that out of God's tender heart for His creation, He set aside a day for the Israelites to rest and trust Him completely. What joy it has been for my family to rest by faith, along with the great cloud of witnesses that have gone before us.

In our Sabbath journey as a family, we have been mentored by some great writers, notably Marva Dawn. Her book *Keeping the Sabbath Wholly* is one you should probably pick up. You can actually just stop reading this, and go get hers. Let her teach you her ways.

One arresting thought she had for me in my motherhood was, "Setting aside a holy Sabbath means that we can cease our productivity and accomplishments for one day in every seven. The exciting thing about such a practice is that it changes our attitudes for the rest of the week. It frees us up to worry less about how much we produce the other days. I desperately need to keep the Sabbath so that this attitude can increasingly pervade the rest of my days."—Marva Dawn

Ceasing productivity and accomplishments felt like life on the floor, with nothing to show but connecting with and enjoying my children. Sabbath is a call to play instead of produce. Sabbath frees me to cease striving, to cease seeing others according to what they produce, to cease finding my value in my productivity. Sabbath is such a gift!

I have taken to starting my Sabbath with Isaiah 43:1–4, reminding me I am valuable because I am loved by God and because I am delighted in by our King. Not because of anything I produce or by some sparkling performance:

Fear not, for I
have redeemed you;
I have called you by name, you are mine.
When you pass through the waters, I will be with you;
and through the rivers, they shall not overwhelm you;
when you walk through fire you shall not be burned,
and the flame shall not consume you.
For I am the Lord your God,
the Holy One of Israel, your Savior.
I give Egypt as your ransom,
Cush and Seba in exchange for you.
Because you are precious in my eyes,
and honored, and I love you...

I don't have a checklist to show at the end of my Sabbath, and it sustains my soul. It heals the hurry. It binds up the broken-rushing-around that is my life. And the proven fact in my life is that I sleep better on the night before the Sabbath. Grace has arrived, and it has come with peaceful sleep. Even to lay our head on our pillow and to shut it all down, this is by faith. We are choosing to trust that God is in control. We sleep by faith.

I can think of no human more in need of knowing they can sabbath and cease from productivity than a mother. To know they can be slow and deliberate. To know they can rest intentionally, embrace nature, and feast with friends and family.

By God's grace, I have seen my Sunday Night Dread turn around. By the time it's Sunday evening, I am rested and absolutely ready to get to work. The rest has recharged me and even ushered in an eagerness to get to the new week, with a full tank and a full heart.

If we keep our chin up, He rains down grace. He provides for us, and may have already provided for us, and will simply remind us where it is. God was providing the material for a speaking engagement months before, because He knew. He knew my need to rest. He knew my naps. He knew how hard it would be to not work.

I was able to find time on the Tuesday before the Thursday to finalize my talk. I have never put together a talk to a group of 150 college students just two days before the event. Usually prepared and practiced by then, I was in a different spot. Because of my rest and trust, my preparation was easy and light. Fun even! I enjoyed waiting to see how God was going to orchestrate the words and use it for His glory.

Stepping off the stage that evening, several women were hoping to talk more about my content and had a story to share of their own. But the greatest gift wasn't how lives were affected that evening; it was how my faith grew from trusting Jesus to provide. I have drawn on that specific Sabbath many times since, especially when I remember something I have to do that I don't feel ready for on the Sabbath. I breathe, remember how God provided that talk, and rest my soul again. Some Sabbaths this is an hourly practice. Some Sabbaths come much easier. It keeps me connected to God and remembering His promises and provision. Sabbath is such a soul-healer.

Chin up, Mommas. We can truly cease trying to prove ourselves and embrace God's provision.

Femininity is not just lipstick, stylish hairdos, and trendy clothes. It is the divine adornment of humanity. It finds expression in your qualities of your capacity to love, your spirituality, delicacy, radiance, sensitivity, creativity, charm, graciousness, gentleness, dignity, and quiet strength.

—James E. Faust

16

How Fitting

Does motherhood always fit perfectly on me now? Please, sister.

But does grace look amazing on me?

YES.

Everyone looks great in grace. Never met anyone who couldn't wear it. Sometimes I put on rules, my own strength, my best perfectionism. But it's not all that becoming, and it's pretty revealing. Often you can see right through it.

Grace is like wearing Spiritual Spanx. Grace covers everything and keeps it classy. It's the perfect fit for any mom. The Designer is brilliant and truly has our best interest in mind. This has become my spiritual infomercial: Motherhood looks awesome on us when we are donned in God's grace.

Motherhood fits beautifully when I see myself in His image, sustaining like Him. This also goes for creating (artists, entrepreneurs, musicians, etc.), consummating (educators, parenting, pastoring, etc.), and redeeming (medicine, counseling, law) too. Professor Stevens taught me that all jobs fit somewhere in these four categories: sustaining, creating, consummating, or redeeming. Don't think that one job is more spiritual or significant than another. All have meaning and purpose and are in the image of God.

Which brings us to the best fit in motherhood: How you were made. Your gifts look great on you. Stop trying on everyone else's gifts. Wear yours. Have at it as you design, make music, write, encourage, bake, lead, teach, care, love. You are designed in God's image. If you have orphaned dreams, please find them again. Even if it's just to dust them off and get a good look at 'em. Now may not be the time, but don't abandon them forever. Dreams may be dormant for a season, but they aren't dead.

God's grace, strength, and dignity are stunning on our motherhood-dress. And trusting God—that's gorgeous. These days I practice whispering, "God I trust you with this." I trust Him with getting those ridiculously rubbery dresses back on the Disney princesses. What is WITH those dresses? I am sweating and pulling and trying so hard to smile while my daughter waits for the wardrobe change. These dresses represent how impossible playing can feel to me, how motherhood can feel. But I walk through the valley of the shadow of dresses. And I trust that whatever my task at hand—it will be for good. Or for my sanctification. Or for humility. For connecting to God and His grace. For all those combined.

Playing with Legos and dolls isn't my strength, but I still get low, get giggling, get humble. I still choose to participate in the puzzles and do so by faith. Trusting that it's not about the puzzles, it's about the people. About being next to my child. The shared space and little hands and sweet kisses in between each piece. I've given myself freedom to not love certain things and do them anyway. We all have our vegetables in motherhood. We may not love them going down, but we see how they nourish our lives.

I whisper, "God I trust you" when I look back and see sin, mistakes, and broken moments in my life and in my motherhood. When I've yelled and seen their saucer eyes and how they were afraid. How it scared me and scared them. How those moments broke me and I was at the end of my rope, at the end of myself. I am trusting God in the small and in the severe. I trust Him that His love covers all shame, His grace covers all sin. All means all.

Because the whole entire thing is this: I can trust

God's grace instead of myself.

I can trust God will use my lack of loving playing dolls and my mistakes and my issues and my sin for growth, for maturity (both in me or my children) and for good. Because God causes everything to work together for good for those who love Him, to be more like His Son.

We can watch God's grace show up when we don't want to. We can trust God's grace will cause growth in the dry places. We can lean on God's grace instead of lunging for control. We can bank on God's grace to rebuild broken places. We can lift up our chin and trust that God's grace is higher:

> *For my thoughts are not your thoughts,*
> *neither are your ways my ways, declares the Lord.*
> *For as the heavens are higher than the earth,*
> *so are my ways higher than your ways*
> *and my thoughts than your thoughts.*
> *—Isaiah 55: 8–9*

Some days my dress still feels like it's exposing things I wanted carefully covered up. But I keep my chin up and believe God's grace will beautifully cover over my flaws and unraveled soul. I remind myself I live among a community committed to grace-giving. We can even boast in our exposure, because God's grace is enough. Let's get low, get grateful, get grace-filled together, friend.

Chin up, hold your beautiful head high. Grace, strength, and dignity are ravishing on you, darling. God's grace is the perfect fit for motherhood.

From the Author

As for you, you were dead in your transgressions and sins, in which you used to live when you followed the ways of this world and of the ruler of the kingdom of the air, the spirit who is now at work in those who are disobedient. All of us also lived among them at one time, gratifying the cravings of our flesh and following its desires and thoughts. Like the rest, we were by nature deserving of wrath. But because of his great love for us, God, who is rich in mercy, made us alive with Christ even when we were dead in transgressions—it is by grace you have been saved. And God raised us up with Christ and seated us with him in the heavenly realms in Christ Jesus, in order that in the coming ages he might show the incomparable riches of his

grace, expressed in his kindness to us in Christ Jesus. For it is by grace you have been saved, through faith—and this is not from yourselves, it is the gift of God—not by works, so that no one can boast. For we are God's handiwork, created in Christ Jesus to do good works, which God prepared in advance for us to do."
—Ephesians 2: 1–10

The Grace that came down from Heaven is why we have a gift of grace to begin with. God came in the form of a baby, moved into the neighborhood, and lived life on this earth like all of us. He grew up, had siblings, parents, a job, and a mission. Jesus came and lived a perfect life on earth—something incredibly hard to wrap my mind around—taught stunning truths, and healed broken people. In his teaching, He said He was equal to God, and this is what got Him crucified. But it was all planned out from the beginning—from Eden. He chose this path, and we participated. When everything broke and sin flooded the earth, we were left up a creek without a paddle. Jesus became our Paddle, our Rescuer, our Bridge back to God. We deserved death, yet He took our place. His death paid the ransom we could not afford.

But then.

Three dark days later, the tomb was empty and

Jesus was very much alive. He ate fish and hugged friends. He was resurrected. Jesus defeated sin and death—and those who believe in Him are made alive, just like that! All who believe in Him, and what He has done, have the right to become children of God.

This is the gift of grace that covers everything: His grace covers our sin, it covers our shame, it covers our issues, it covers our motherhood. It is by grace that we have been saved, by faith in Jesus, not by our own works.

Friends, Jesus is who I adore and stand in awe of. His life, His teaching, His gift of grace through the cross. And He invites every single person to believe in Him and know His grace. Just tell Him you need Him. May you know the Giver of the grace that covers all. All means all.

Acknowledgments

There is a sweet team of people called "The Staff Team" at Brookside Church of which I am a part. Ricky—you and Gelly are some of the biggest cheerleaders I know. With hilarious videos, shared dreams, and real Jesus-grit. Thank you for being awesome. Thank you Ashley. You sat in my car with me when I got a one million page email about how this might not work. You are both saint and sister who sends encouraging texts about my writing. Erin, you have prayed for me, written me strong encouragements, served me with launch team spreadsheets and been the sweetest gift in this process. And pedis are the best with you. Sara, a friend first then a co-worker— thank you. You keep me grounded and don't care that I always have many ideas and would kindly tell me my blurbs for the church program were novels. Touché. Love you. Sam, you were the brave one. The lone man who stepped on this ride and gave edits and critique and a manly, non-mom, brilliant view. Thank you for your time and your mind. Craig, because not only did I slide down the walls in laughter in the office for who knows what, but because you have a fierce belief in me. You listened to God and passed it on, and here we are. Thank you for walking with Jesus. Steve, because the years in ministry have added up and the actual truth is that your thoughts are what wrote half of this book. You have deposited truths, concepts, parables, and a way of thinking about Jesus that helped put it all together. Thank you. Kevin, because the day I cried in my car, you had planned to ask me to do a mother's day sermon. Which turned into this entire book. You've been a big brother and a generous leader in the process and I'm so thankful.

To those who hopped on my book-writing-cheering-team, and are in general amazing, loyal friends. Sandy, thank you for being a lifelong friend and a compass. Jenn, you have lent me skirts and bravery and listening ears. Who attends conferences, but not really? You, girl. Eternally grateful. Libby, you told me years ago you would be pumped to read a book of mine. You have a fierce loyalty and a loud cheer—thank you. Gelly, you don't care how many subtitles I send you. You never tire of being in it. You've been a marketer, truth-bomber, and a grace-girl. Thank you. Jamie, you keep listening to me, empathizing, encouraging, sitting in it with me. So much life shared and courage infused. You came and sat on the floor with me. Thank you. Lori—because you found it a blast and you call to tell me all the ways you see God's hand in it. You lay down the truth, with laughter in the middle of it all. Let's podcast. It's the best. Trinity, you jumped right in and edited and questioned and refined and laughed. Your English eye and the way you love Jesus, and love me, were a perfect match. Thank you.

To those of you who have given me guidance and wise counsel for years on end: Greg and Sharry—because so much of my dreaming started in your office or in the youth group room or in some van on a mission trip. Love you. Tim—you plus oatmeal equals amazing wisdom, training, and counseling. Thank you for letting me pour it all out there. And for your hard work. Michael—thank you. You believed in me in so many ways and in all sorts of ministry. And you'll always be ten years older and that's the best. Professor Stevens—you opened up my eyes and gave me an entirely new way to see the world. I am so grateful. Martha—because you are hilarious and real and an amazing prayer-warrior and you hear God. And God put you in my backyard and I watched you whisper to your toddler and not yell and it was beautiful. Libby—you are a soul sister in every possible way. I just love you dearly. Bethany—your positive ideas, humor, love, encouragement—so beautiful. Kati—because Mall Madness and wanting to be a mom forever were so you; I love your love of family and traditions and memories.

Natalia. Girl. And I thought I had grit. You're an editing ninja, from the first day I met you. You had your eyes wide open, asking God for what's next. You are ready for any and all adventures and I can clearly see that three boys are your jam for this very reason. You reworked and refined and texted in the middle of an actual hurricane. You not only edited the socks off this book, but you would write and say how much we needed it. Which was the best. Each edited chapter was like Christmas. Thank you.

Mom—because, in SO many ways, motherhood looks great on you. You still love puzzles on the floor and domestic things and sewing phenomenal dresses. You are laid back, full of grace, and ready to laugh. Thank you for being a fantastic mom. Dad—because you said it to begin with. You have a gusto for life. You taught me to keep writing, as you do, and you do things "all in". You are all in with all emotions and ideas and grandkids, and it's great. Thank you.

Holly—because I am tearing up right now thinking about the flowers you sent when I got rejection emails. Because you send hilarious texts. Because you always call with THE best wisdom, and tell me I am actually a writer. You're amazing.

Rob—one of the most attractive things about you is your creativity. Nothing is out. Nothing is too much. Nothing is off the table. I could not have pulled any kind of stunt like writing a book and making it gorgeous without you. Thank you is not enough. But I still mean it. I adore you.

Discussion Questions

Chapter 1:

1. Have you always dreamed of being a mom, or was motherhood a secondary thought to other dreams?

2. What dreams did you have growing up?

3. What speaks to you about Isaiah 40:10–11:

Tell the towns of Judah,
"Your God is coming!"
Yes, the Sovereign Lord is coming in power.
He will rule with a powerful arm.
See, he brings his reward with him as he comes.
He will feed his flock like a shepherd.
He will carry the lambs in his arms,
holding them close to his heart.
He will gently lead the mother sheep with their young.

4. What do you think about the definitions of grace? Do you live like these are true?

Grace: God's favor on the unworthy.

Grace: kindness from God we do not deserve.

Grace: a gift given where nothing is owed in return

Chapter 2

1. Do you like life on the floor? If so, what part of motherhood is hard for you with your kids?
2. Is it hard for you to accept that you are not enough? That even our weakness is a gift?
3. What does it look like to actually boast in your weakness, so that the power of Christ rests on you?

Chapter 3

1. What maintaining and sustaining activity is really hard for you?
2. How do you feel about the idea that maintaining and sustaining are not second class, but just like God?
3. In all honesty, which area of your life is the hardest for you to apply grace to? How are you in offering grace to others? Messy homes? Messy hearts? Messy anything?

Chapter 4

1. Have you divided your life into things that feel spiritual or unspiritual, significant or insignificant?

2. Stevens writes, "In the New Testament 'service' lasts and has significance to God not because of its religious character, but because it is done in faith, hope, and love (1 Cor 3:9–15; 13:13 and 1 Thess 1:3). Sermons may dissolve in the fire of final judgment because they were preached for vain glory, while a sweater knit in love may be a ministry to Jesus (Matthew 25:40)." How do you feel about categories being rearranged to anything done in faith, hope, and love is significant to God?

4. Amy writes, "My life became a level playing field. The significance of my day came from my heart, not my to do list. I knew this on the edges, but it all came into focus for me. Probably because I was thirsty enough to go looking. To get my chin up. To quit naval-gazing and see what God intended for us here on earth." What resonates with you from this?

Chapter 5

1. Amy writes, "You have made your laundry too big and your King too small. With all due respect,

you've elevated yourself too high in your thinking and have placed a mighty God too low in your mind." What does it look like when you make yourself and your problems big, and God small?

2. In the book of Isaiah God feeds, carries, holds and leads you. Which of those four do you need God to do for you today? Have you asked Him?

3. Amy closes with: "Chin up, sister. God is FOR you and He is WITH you. Feeding, carrying, holding, and gently leading you." Do you believe God is for you and that He is with you?

Chapter 6

1. When is the last time you intentionally practiced not accomplishing anything? Or put everything down and simply enjoyed your children?

2. Amy writes, "I had forgotten that my people need my influence. These are God's creations in my home. Budding disciples under my roof. And what does Jesus do with His people, His disciples? He gets low. He serves them. He washes their feet. He gives them intentional, undivided attention. He influences their entire lives with His love." Do you consider your children to be your stage, voice and vision?

3. Do you see yourself as an oak of righteousness, being raised up to raise up others in love?

Chapter 7

1. Amy writes, "If I don't get healthy away from my people, then I can't be healthy with my people. If I step outside of it all and get hope, I can step inside of it all and give love." Have you done some stepping outside of your home to get healthy?

2. If you were to make some changes to be a healthier mom, what would those changes be?

   Amy practices whispering some truths:

   "God, I am so tired, but you never tire. I'm thankful you don't sleep so I can."

   "God, don't let my foot slip. Your word says you won't. I am trusting You."

   "God, you are watching over me. Thank you."

   "God ,you are my help. I need You."

   "God, you are the keeper of my whole day. Be near right now."

   "God, shade me from lies. Keep me in truth."

   Which one do you need to practice today?

Chapter 8

1. Amy shares her first birth experience. What has been a big unmet expectation in your motherhood?

2. Take some time to make an actual list of "Ashes

of Unmet Expectations" and "Crowns of Beauty." What did you find?

3. Amy writes, "Humility connects us to the beauty in motherhood. When we wave our white flag and say we are not enough, we open up a world of beauty. Motherhood is one of the most humbling and beautiful gifts we've been given." How have you seen humility connect you to the beauty of motherhood and to other mothers?

Chapter 9

1. How has anger played a role in your life? In what ways have you experienced it or have you shown your anger?

   "Whoever has no rule over her own spirit is like a city broken down, without walls."
   —Proverbs 25:28

   What hits you about this verse?

2. Can you relate to the Chicken Little story about acorns falling? How do you handle unmet expectations/acorns in your day?

3. A friend recommended the word "bummer" as a way to keep acorns in their proper place. How does this idea sit with you?

Chapter 10

1. What has it looked like as you have had two call-

ings under one roof?

2. Amy identifies three lies about two callings under one roof. Which lie resonates with you the most? Is her truth helpful to you?

3. What gifts do you find in having two callings under one roof?

Chapter 11

1. What has been your experience with depression—either your own or someone close to you?

2. What has been your view on faith and medicine?

3. How does Amy's narrative about depression speak to you?

Chapter 12

1. Martha is a busy servant, wanting to help and open her home. She gets frustrated with Mary who chose to sit at Jesus' feet. What resonates with you from Jesus' response?

2. What do you think about Paul Stevens assessment: "What was so right about Mary's inaction? Very little. What was Jesus' concern? It is more important to let God minister TO us than to minister FOR God."

3. Letting God minister to us vs. ministering for God is a subtle but pivotal distinction. How does this sit with you?

Chapter 13

1. Amy offers a big picture roadmap from Eve to Mary. What reactions do you have about this?
2. How do you feel about being in the same stream of motherhood as Eve and Mary?
3. Do you see God's grace in the metanarrative of the Bible? How do you see God's grace over your life?

Chapter 14

1. How do you feel about Amy's story with her foster child singing about bravery?
2. What has been your experience or thoughts about foster care?
3. Amy talked through "all means all." How does this hit you for today?

   God is able to make all grace abound to you, so that having all sufficiency in all things at all times, you may abound in every good work.
   —2 Corinthians 9:8

4. Amy writes about orphaned children and orphaned dreams. What does this concept look like in your life?

Chapter 15

1. Do you get the Sunday Night Dreads and the Monday Morning Blues?

2. After reading this chapter, what are your thoughts on taking a weekly Sabbath?

3. Does it feel scary to stop for one whole entire day, each week? Why?

4. John Piper puts it this way: "Jesus didn't come to abolish the Sabbath but to dig it out from under the mountain of legalistic sediment, and give it to us again as a blessing rather than a burden." Do you see the Sabbath as a blessing or a burden? Why do you think so?

Chapter 16

1. Amy used a dress analogy throughout the book. Do you believe that grace looks great on everyone?

2. Where is it hard to believe that God's grace is enough in your motherhood?

3. What is your biggest takeaway from this book?

Notes

Chapter 1

"Good Morning Quote", accessed April 28, 2017, https://www.goodmorningquote.com/mother-daughter-quotes/

"Values.Com", accessed June 15, 2017, https://www.values.com/inspirational-quotes/3728-experience-that-most-brutal-of-teachers-but

Chapter 2

"Meryl Streep Quotes," Brainy Quotes, accessed, September 15, 2017, https://www.brainyquote.com/quotes/quotes/m/merylstree135057.html

"Brene Brown Quote", The Guardian, accessed, September 15, 2017, https://www.theguardian.com/lifeandstyle/2013/jul/27/brene-brown-people-sick-being-afraid

Chapter 3

"Timothy Keller Quotes," Quote Fancy, accessed September 15, 2017, https://quotefancy.com/quote/921593/Timothy-Keller-God-invites-us-to-come-as-we-are-not-stay-as-we-are

Robert Banks and R. Paul Stevens, The Complete Book of Everyday Christianity, (Downers Grove: InterVarsity Press, 1997), Elizabeth Dryer quote, 76

Chapter 4

"C.S.Lewis Quotes," Deseret News, accessed Sept 15, 2017, https://www.deseretnews.com/top/817/0/Top-100-CS-Lewis-quotes-.html

R. Paul Stevens. "Ministry." The Complete Book of Everyday Christianity, eds. Robert Banks and R. Paul Stevens (Downers Grove: InterVarsity Press, 1977) 633-641

Chapter 5

"Lord Byron Quotes," Quote HD, accessed Sept 15, 2017, http://www.quotehd.com/quotes/lord-byron-quote-letter-writing-is-the-only-device-for-combining-solitude-with

Chapter 6

"Brene Brown Quotes," Goodreads, accessed Sept 15, 2017, https://www.goodreads.com/author/quotes/162578.Bren_Brown?page=36

"George Washington Quotes", BrainyQuotes, https://www.brainyquote.com/quotes/quotes/g/georgewash118444.html

Chapter 7
"Quote by Sheila Walsh," Goodreads, accessed Sept 15, 2017, https://www.goodreads.com/quotes/824635-my-brokenness-is-a-better-bridge-for-people-than-my

Chapter 8
"Ralph Waldo Emerson Quotes," Brainy Quotes, accessed Sept 15, 2017, http://www.quotehd.com/quotes/lord-byron-quote-letter-writing-is-the-only-device-for-combining-solitude-with
"Jen Hatmaker Sermons," Willow Creek Sermons, accessed Oct 28, 2017, https://willowcreek.tv/sermons/south-barrington/2015/05/mothers-day

Chapter 9
"Henry Nouwen Quotes", Brainy Quotes, accessed Sept 15, 2017, https://www.brainyquote.com/quotes/quotes/h/henrinouwe588351.html
"Ralph Waldo Emerson Quotes," Good Reads, accessed Sept 15, 2017, https://www.goodreads.com/quotes/353-for-every-minute-you-are-angry-you-lose-sixty-seconds
Gregory L. Jantz, "Controlling Your Anger Before It Controls You" (Grand Rapids, MI: Revell a division of Baker Publishing Group, 2013) 376, iBooks

Chapter 10
"Shauna Niequist Quotes", Qideas, accessed September 15, 2017, http://qideas.org/videos/what-i-learned-from-my-mother/
Ecclesiastes 1:14

Chapter 11
Page Quote, Exodus 14:10-14, NIV, Zondervan, 2011
"StrengthsFinders Competition", Leadership Vision Consulting, accessed September 20, 2017, http://www.leadershipvisionconsulting.com/how-the-strengthsfinder-theme-of-competition-can-be-generative/

Chapter 12
"C.S Lewis Quotes," Goodreads, accessed Sept 15, 2017, "Though our feelings come and go, God's love for us does not." - C.S. Lewis
Paul Stevens, INDS/SPIR 578 Everyday Spirituality Continuuing Studies Course, 2003

Chapter 13
"Spiritual Motherhood Quotes" Pinterest, accessed September 30, 2017, https://za.pinterest.com/pin/374854368960165899/?lp=true

Chapter 14
"Rita Pierson Quotes," The Picta, accessed Sept 15, 2017, http://www.thepicta.com/tag/ritapierson
"Robin Williams Quotes," Brainy Quote, accessed Sept 15, 2017, https://www.brainyquote.com/quotes/quotes/r/robinwilli383827.html

Chapter 15
"Eugene Peterson Quotes," Faith On Campus, accessed Sept 15, 2017, http://faithoncampus.com/blog/eugene-peterson-on-sabbath/
Marva Dawn, "Keeping the Sabbath Wholly" (Grand Rapids, Eerdmans Publishing Co., Zondervan, 2002) 19

Chapter 16
"James E. Faust Quotes," Brainy Quotes, accessed Sept 15, 2017, https://www.brainyquote.com/quotes/authors/j/james_e_faust.html

52133147R00116

Made in the USA
Middletown, DE
16 November 2017